Cognitive Behavioral Therapy Made Simple

Effective Strategies to Rewire Your Brain and Instantly Overcome Depression, End Anxiety, Manage Anger, and Stop Panic Attacks in its Tracks.

(Change Your Life Series, Book 2)

By

Charles P. Carlton

Dr. Lee Henton

Copyright © 2020 – Charles P. Carlton & Dr. Lee Henton

No part of this publication may be reproduced, distributed, or transmitted in any form or by any means, including photocopying, recording, or other electronic or mechanical methods, without the prior written permission of the publisher, except in the case of brief quotations embodied in reviews and certain other non-commercial uses permitted by copyright law.

Disclaimer

This publication is designed to provide reliable information on the subject matter only for educational purposes, and it is not intended to provide medical advice for any medical treatment. You should always consult your doctor or physician for guidance before you stop, start, or alter any prescription medications or attempt to implement the methods discussed. This book is published independently by the author and has no affiliation with any brands or products mentioned within it. The author hereby disclaims any responsibility or liability whatsoever that is incurred from the use or application of the contents of this publication by the purchaser or reader. The purchaser or reader is hereby responsible for his or her own actions.

Books By The Same Authors

Books By Charles P. Carlton

How to Stop Overthinking (Change Your Life Series, Book 1)
Master Your Emotions (2 Books in 1)
Stop Overthinking and Vagus Nerve Stimulation
(2 Books in 1)

Books By Dr. Lee Henton

The Secrets of Vagus Nerve Stimulation
Vagus Nerve Stimulation and CBT Made Simple
(2 Books in 1)
The 5-Minutes DIY Homemade Hand Sanitizer
The 10-Minutes DIY Homemade Face Mask
Homemade Hand Sanitizer and Homemade Face Mask
(2 Books In 1)
The Budget-Friendly Renal Diet Cookbook

Table of Contents

Books By The Same Authors 2
Free Gift 7
About Charles 7
About Lee 10
Introduction 11
Charles's Story 16
Section I 19
Understanding Cognitive Behavioral Therapy 19
Chapter 1 20
What is CBT? 20
   A Short Trip Down History 23
   How Does CBT Work? 26
      CBT is About Meanings 27
      Where Do These Negative Thoughts Come From? 32
      CBT as a Doing Therapy 33
   Who Can CBT Help? 35
   CBT Principles – What is CBT Like? 37
   How Effective is CBT? 39
   How is CBT Administered? 44
   What Types of CBT Are There? 49
   Pros and Cons of CBT 58
Chapter 2 61
What Does CBT Involve? 61
   Step 1: Identifying the Problem and Setting Goals 61
   Step 2: Identifying Core Beliefs About the Problems 63

What are Core Beliefs? 63
How Core Beliefs Develop 64
Identifying Core Beliefs 66
Step 3: Analyzing Core Beliefs by Identifying Cognitive
Distortions 72
What are Cognitive Distortions? 73
Types of Cognitive Distortions 74
Steps to Identifying Cognitive Distortions 79
Step 4: Cognitive Restructuring or Challenging Your
Negative Automatic Thoughts 81
Finding the Objective Truth About the Thoughts 83
Making the Restructured Thoughts Habitual 87
Step 5: Monitor Your Feelings 88
Exercise 90
Section II 93
Cognitive Behavioral Therapy Strategies 93
Chapter 3 94
CBT for Depression 94
Understanding Depression 94
Symptoms of Depression 95
Causes & Diagnosis 96
CBT Treatment for Depression 97
What Keeps Depression Going? 99
Behavioral Theory of Depression 100
Cognitive Theory of Depression 102
CBT Technique for Depression 103
Behavioral Activation 103
Exercise 1 106

    Exercise 2 107
    Exercise 3 111
    Exercise 4 114
  Mindfulness 117
  Vagus Nerve Stimulation Therapy 119

Chapter 4 121
CBT for Anxiety 121
Understanding Anxiety, Worry, and Fear 121
Symptoms of Anxiety 123
Causes & Diagnosis 123
CBT Treatment for Anxiety 124
  Exposure Therapy 127
    Practicing Exposure Therapy More Effectively 132
      Removal of Safety Signals 139
      Multiple Contexts 140
      Retrieval Cues 141
  Relaxation Training 142
  Complementary Therapy for Anxiety 149
  Panic Attacks 150
    What Causes Panic Attacks? 151
    What Keeps Panic Attacks Going? 153
    Treatment Options for Panic Attacks 155
    Interoceptive Exposure 156
      Step One: Pick a Trigger 160
      Step Two: Create a Fear Hierarchy 161
      Step Three: Rate the Hierarchy 161
      Step Four: Starting Exposure 163
      Step Five: Middle Sessions of Exposure 164

    Step Six: Ending Exposure 165
        Exercise 165
Chapter 5 177
CBT for Anger Management 177
  What is Anger? 177
  Angry Thoughts, Behaviors, and Physical Symptoms ... 178
  The Cycle of Anger – How Anger Develops.................... 179
  Causes of Anger 180
  Cost of Anger 182
  Myths & Facts About Anger.................................... 183
  CBT Treatment for Anger 184
    Ellis's A-B-C-D Technique 185
      A = Activating Event....................................... 186
      B = Belief System 186
      C = Consequences 186
      D = Dispute 187
      Exercise 190
Conclusion 194
References 197

Free Gift

In expression of my gratitude for purchasing my book, I am offering you a free copy of my *Bulletproof Self-Esteem* companion guide, proven to boost your self-confidence in **ONE WEEK**.

To have instant access to this gift, type this link http://bit.ly/346qi8P into your web browser, or you can send an email to charlescarltonpublishing@gmail.com, and I would get your copy across to you.

About Charles

Charles P. Carlton, a former consultant with a top big 4 global consulting firm, Ernst & Young and a Fortune 100 best companies to work for is a self-help professional, devoted to showing you the tricks on how to hack your life to get the most out of it by getting things done.

His quest for self-discovery led him to retire from the corporate world to fulfil his life-long goals of being a self-help coach and writer.

He specializes in using a cut-through science-based and personal experience approach in connecting with his audience in areas of emotional intelligence, self-esteem, and self-confidence, self-discovery, communication, personal development, and productivity. This has helped him build successful relationships and connections with his audience.

When not writing, Charles loves reading and exploring

the beauty of nature from where most times he gets many thought-provoking inspirations.

About Lee

Dr. Lee Henton is a US-trained General Practice Doctor from the Johns Hopkins University School of Medicine with additional qualification in nutritional medicine from Iowa State University. He is a certified specialist in dietology and nutrition.

He has extensive years of medical and nutritional experience across general medicine, pediatrics, traumatology, addictions, food nutrition, and diet therapy.

He currently runs a co-established private medical and wellness practice where he operates from. His approach is personalized with each client by combining medical and food nutrition counseling. All advice he provides is at par with his experience, as well as with medical and nutritional concepts. He specializes primarily in men and women's health.

He lives in Minnesota with his wife and two daughters.

Introduction

We've all found ourselves being overcome by the firm grip of overwhelming emotions at some point. This could be a feeling of depression that paints life with a gloomy color, dreadful anxiety, excessive anger, panic attacks that strike without warning, or perhaps, other feelings that forcefully overtakes our hearts and minds. When we are emotionally thrown off balance by these feelings, it becomes paramount that we take conscious and intentional steps toward regaining strength to find relief as soon as possible – preventing any further wreckage being done to our overall mental health and wellbeing. During the late stages of my emotional breakdown episode and in my quest for emotional freedom, I came across a unique but fascinating treatment option that seemed quite different from other types of treatments for people who suffered from depression, anxiety, and panic attacks. This treatment option is called cognitive behavioral therapy (CBT). The more I dug deeper into this therapy and its inner workings, the more I realized how depression, anxiety, anger and panic overtake our thoughts, plunging it into harmful directions, and how CBT can help to retrain our thoughts in serving us better. I also learned that when we build more activities into our daily lives that are not only rewarding but fun, they tend to have very powerful antidepressant effects. 'Being present' with positive curiosity and openness, I discovered, is one of the most powerful ways you can break free from anxiety and depression. This approach, the mindfulness-based method, has received wide acceptance and is backed by sufficient research as the "third wave" of CBT, including other cognitive and behavioral techniques.

I have observed that when we are fighting the battle to win back our emotional and mental wellbeing, we usually lack the time, willingness, and energy to go through pages of research findings to find what can work for the given situation. We need straight to the point treatment options that can be used right away. However the case, they are not easy to follow through with as I have learned that even while these treatment options are effective and simple to apply, they do require an amount of work and effort. This is particularly hard to do when you are depressed and demotivated, or when you are fighting back panic attacks. This is where the power of CBT comes into play, providing you with a goal to work toward, as well as carefully designed step by step techniques to help you get there.

As much as possible, I have strived to ensure that the succeeding chapters of this book are simplistic, engaging, and helpful to enable you to overcome your current emotional dilemma. Also, this book has been designed to serve those who haven't heard of CBT, those who currently work with a therapist, or who have made use of CBT in the past but need a new resource as a refresher for up to date information.

At the end of this book, you will;

- Have a better understanding of what CBT means.

- Understand how your thoughts determine your feelings and behaviors.
- Discover science-backed research why CBT is a very effective therapeutic option in the treatment of depression, anxiety, anger, and panic attacks.
- Be more aware of what you must do to ensure you get the most out of CBT.
- Be enlightened on how the negative thoughts that fuel your negative emotions develop, and how you can identify them when they come to mind.
- Uncover life hacks that you can apply right away to challenge and replace your negative thoughts with more balanced, healthy, and rational thoughts.
- Know how to make your new, restructured thoughts your second nature, and how to monitor your feelings to prevent a relapse.
- Discover tailored and proven techniques you can start right now and how you can apply them to overcome depression, end anxiety,

- manage anger, and stop panic attacks in its tracks.
- Begin your journey toward reclaiming your overall health and mental wellbeing with the aid of the carefully structured case studies and practice exercises to guide you along the way.

…and much more!

In conclusion, I am very thrilled to not only share my personal story and struggle with depression, anxiety, and anger but most importantly, I am excited to provide you with a simplistic but yet detailed guide that will truly make your understanding of CBT worthwhile. I hope you find this book really helpful so that nothing gets in your way of living the life you enjoy and love.

Charles's Story

I was moved to write this book, which is my latest work due to my personal experience on the subject and how much so I got fascinated about Cognitive Behavioral Therapy (CBT), especially as it focuses on thinking patterns and how the thoughts we think shape our lives, as it did me. On Friday, January 4th, 2018, to be precise, I lost my job after many years of being a committed and high performing employee. If only losing my job was all I had to deal with, but it isn't. Month after month, I went on a downward spiral of one financial loss or the other due to bad monetary decisions, leaving me bankrupt from my years of hard work and savings – all in a bid to stay afloat until my next job comes. But the next job wasn't near in sight, and never came. To cap it up, I lost my mother to the cold hands of death, a mother I found great comfort in during times of difficulties, a mother I could share my problems with without feeling judged, a mother who gave me joy and a reason to keep pressing on through the travails of life, a mother who loved me unconditionally, a mother unreplaceable.

All these experiences made 2018 the worst year of my life, to say the least. I was depressed, experienced severe anxiety about everything, angry at life, and at having not only failed myself but my mother, who sacrificed so much to see me succeed in life. This even made me feel more emptiness, hopeless, lonely, and sad for 12 tough months. Though it seemed short, you may say, but it was the longest year of my life. I also developed suicidal tendencies and wished that death could come sooner. My depression became really bad that it dawned on me on December 1st, 2018, that I needed to get help from a therapist. Although the sessions I had with the therapist was an eye-opener on how much I had allowed my mistakes, failures, and losses to shape my way of thinking, how much I saw myself in a negative light, and how much all that happened isn't entirely my fault, I realized, however, that the ultimate power to reframe my negative thinking pattern into a more positive one lied with me. I also needed a strong reason why I needed to persevere through such tough times, a reason why I needed to win the battle for my mental health and wellbeing, and that reason came from the strength of my mother.

It is with this newfound realization that led me to journey on the road to recovery and today, having regained total control of my thoughts, feelings, and behaviors as well as my deep interest on the subject of CBT, I believe it is fair that I shared with you much of what I learned on the road to recovery as I know most of you reading this are probably going through a similar experience. To embark on this journey with me, I have enlisted the assistance of my friend, Dr. Lee Henton, a seasoned medical practitioner with broad knowledge on the subject of CBT as we share invaluable and life-saving hacks that could help you on your way to recovery, as well help a therapist or a counselor in their profession.

See you on the other side!

Section I

Understanding Cognitive Behavioral Therapy

Chapter 1

What is CBT?

Chances are you have heard of cognitive behavioral therapy (CBT), even if you are relatively unfamiliar with psychology. CBT is a common type of talk therapy that is globally practiced and very well used in the treatment of a wide range of conditions and mental health problems such as anxiety, depression, sleeping difficulties, drug, and alcohol abuse, and panic attacks among others – children, adolescents, adults, and older adults can all benefit from it.

In a lay man's term, CBT is based on the idea that how we think (cognition), how we feel (emotion) and how we act (behavior) are all interconnected. Specifically, what we think will determine our feelings and our behavior.

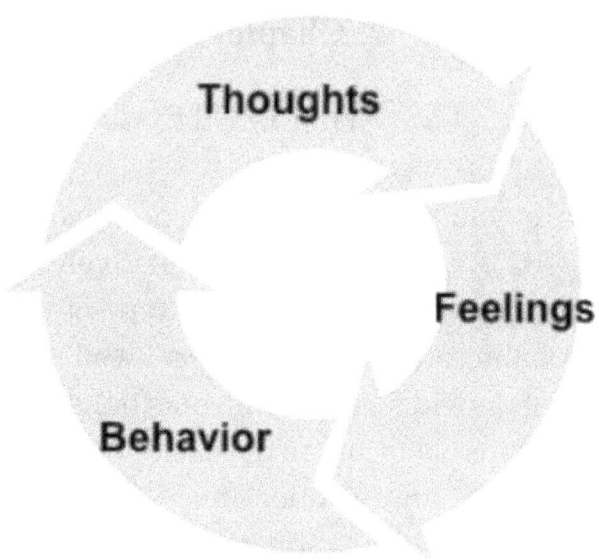

Figure 1: CBT Model

Cognitive Therapy

Cognitive therapy places emphasis on people's thoughts and how these thoughts affect their emotional, behavioral, and physiological responses to stressful situations. Often times, people have difficulty thinking rationally when they feel stressed and pressured by disturbing life experiences. Through cognitive therapy, you can identify and confront your thoughts about yourself, about the people around you, as well as the world around you.

Behavioral Therapy

In its most basic state, behavioral therapy is the encouragement of "patients to engage in adaptive behaviors and not to allow pathological internal experiences to dictate how they act" (Association for Behavioral and Cognitive Therapies, 2012). A person's negative reactions to normal stimuli are typically indicative of learned behaviors; this is because something negative occurred the last time the stimulus was present. Following a process known as extinction, therapists often try to change a person's negative reactions by letting them know that the negative result does not always happen with the stimulus. By following this process, the individual will more than likely positively engage in activities and behaviors if they have previously had positive outcomes. If the results of their activities and behaviors have been negative, then they are less likely to repeat such.

In most cases, psychotherapists who adopt the use of CBT in their practice often personalize and customize the therapy to suit the needs and personality of each person in their care. Have you ever interacted with a mental health therapist, a counselor, or even a psychiatry clinician in a professional setting? Then more than likely, you have participated in CBT. Perhaps your friends, families or loved ones have talked to you about how a mental health professional helped them in identifying unhelpful thoughts, patterns and behaviors, and how they were able to alter them to work towards their goals more effectively, then you have likewise, heard of the impacts of CBT.

In the list of tools used by psychologists when interacting with patients, CBT is one of such tools most frequently used. Though based on simple principles, the outcomes can be wildly positive when put into practice.

In this book, we will take a deeper dive into CBT, its inner workings, and how its principles, among many others, can be applied to improve your life. From this point on, I encourage you to keep a personal journal by your side as you continue reading to document your thoughts and responses as may be required.

A Short Trip Down History

To really understand the approach of cognitive behavioral therapy, it is important to know where it started from and in what reaction it was developed for. CBT emerged in the 1960s, in an era when psychological therapies were less known and practiced than they are today. Aaron T. Beck, a psychiatrist, is popularly credited as being the pioneer of CBT. However, the history of CBT would be incomplete without the mention of Albert Ellis, who, like Aaron Beck, was also developing a form of cognitive therapy at the same time as Beck. Ellis's work later became known as Rational Emotive Behavior Therapy (REBT).

At the time Aaron Beck discovered CBT, he was doing psychoanalysis, working at the University of Pennsylvania in the 1960s. During one of his many analytical sessions with his patients, Aaron observed that his patients displayed tendencies of **internal dialogue** going on in their minds — almost as though they were talking to themselves, but only reporting a fraction of this kind of thinking to him. For example, in a therapy session, the patient, thinking to herself, would mutter internally: "He (Aaron Beck) has not said much to me today. I wonder if he is angry with me?" These thoughts tend to create discomfort with the patient, making the patient feel a little bit anxious or perhaps annoyed. He or she could then respond to this thought with another thought: "He is likely tired, or perhaps I have not been talking about the things that are most important." The second thought most likely might change how the patient was feeling. Observing this with some of his patients, Beck realized that the link between *thoughts* and *feelings* was very important, which resulted in his invention of the term, **automatic thoughts** to describe emotion-filled thoughts that may pop up in the mind. Beck discovered that people were not always aware of such thoughts, but could, however, learn to identify and report them when they arise. Beck found that being able to identify these thoughts was the missing link to the patient understanding and overcoming his/ her problems or difficulties. It is because of the importance that was placed on thoughts that led Beck to call it cognitive therapy, which is now widely known as cognitive behavioral therapy (CBT) simply because the therapy uses behavioral techniques as well. CBT has since then, recorded successful scientific trials in several places by different teams, and has been applied to a variety of health problems.

Simultaneously, Albert Ellis was also working on a form of cognitive therapy that descended from the Stoic idea that it is not events that causes us distress, but the meaning we attribute to them. His ideas were developed as REBT. Although there is a huge overlap between both forms of therapy, Beckian cognitive therapy is unarguably the most influential and widely used form of therapy in the modern world.

How Does CBT Work?

CBT is a goal-oriented psychotherapy treatment that uses a practical, hands-on approach to problem-solving. CBT aims to change the thinking patterns and behaviors that are behind the difficulties people face, and by so doing, changing the way they feel. To change people's thinking patterns and their behaviors, CBT focuses on the thoughts, beliefs, attitudes, and images that are held (the cognitive processes of a person) and how these processes relate to how a person behaves, as a way of dealing with emotional problems.

It is noteworthy to mention that CBT is not designed for lifelong participation, but instead as a short term based therapy aimed to help people meet their goals in the near future. Most CBT treatment lasts somewhere around five to ten months, with patients attending a session per week, and with each session lasting for about 50 to 60-minute. During this time, the patient and therapist are working in collaboration to understand the underlying problems and developing new strategies for tackling them. A set of principles are introduced to the patients through CBT, which they can apply whenever they feel the need to, and that will last them for a lifetime.

For CBT to be effective, the therapist and the patient must both be invested in the process and willing to participate actively – which implies that both the therapist and the patient would need to work as a team to identify the problems the patient is facing, and come up with strategies to address them to create meaningful and positive solutions.

CBT is About Meanings

CBT is based on a model that it is not events in itself that makes us upset, but the meanings we attribute to them. As we live our lives, we interpret what goes on around us by forming *beliefs* and *understandings*. These meanings then go on to affect how we perceive the world. Take, for instance, if our thoughts are too negative, it can prevent us from doing things or seeing things that do not fit, that disconfirm what we believe to be true. In other words, we continue to cling on to the same old thoughts, failing to learn anything new.

Let's represent this analogy using an example. A depressed woman may say to herself, "I can not face going to work today: I just can't do it. Nothing will go right. I'll feel very awful." As a result of having and believing these thoughts, she may well ring in sick. By acting in such a way, she is not allowing herself to find out that her prediction might be wrong. She could have found some other things that she could do, that were at least okay, instead, she stays at home, brooding over her failure to go to work, and ending up thinking: "I have let everyone down. They will be mad at me. Why can't I do just as everyone else does? I'm too weak and worthless." She then ends up most probably feeling very worse, and having even more difficulty going to work the following day. Thinking, behaving, and feeling in such a way like this could trigger the start of a downward spiral. Note that this vicious thought circle applies to several kinds of problems and negative thoughts encountered in our everyday lives.

The figure below paints an illustration of how we give meanings to events and the outcome that results.

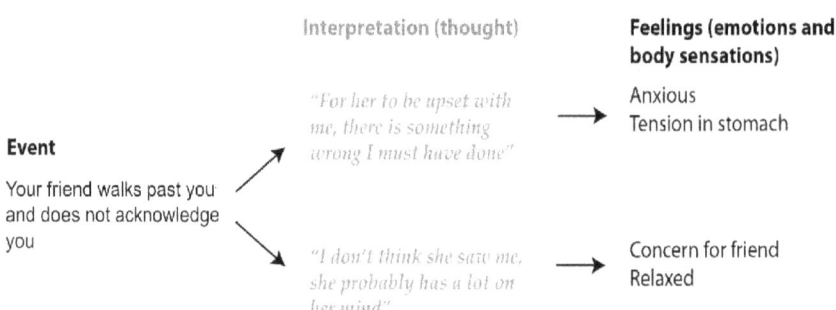

Figure 2: Our interpretation of events determines our feelings toward them.

In the first interpretation, the events are personalized (*"What have I done wrong?"*), which then results in feelings of anxious sensations. However, the second interpretation tends to understand the friend's behavior in a more neutral term, resulting in a different outcome from the first interpretation.

Take a look at another example below

Figure 3: Another example of how our interpretation of events determines how we feel about them.

The first interpretation (the offer of promotion) is an excited one – which is viewed as a welcome opportunity. The second interpretation, however, is less exciting and positive – the person offered a promotion is making a negative prediction of what is likely to happen, resulting in anxiety.

The idea of how we interpret events did not start today. Nearly 2000 years ago, Epictetus, the Greek philosopher said:

"Men are disturbed, not by things, but by the principles and notions which they form concerning things." —**Epictetus**

In 1602, Shakespeare said something similar:

"There is nothing either good or bad, but thinking makes it so." —Shakespeare

How we interpret events may not be a new idea; however, it is a powerful one. It explains why some people are excited at the opportunity singing in front of a crowd (*"At last, my talent will be recognized!"*) whereas, for some other persons, it is a terrifying feeling (*"I will make a fool of myself and everyone will laugh at me!"*).

We may not always be able to change the situations we find ourselves in (or perhaps the people we meet); however, we are responsible and in charge of how we interpret events. How we decide to handle a situation, and the perspective we choose to take would determine how we feel. That being said, have at the back of your mind that CBT may not provide a cure to your condition or make an unpleasant situation go away, but it most definitely can give you the power that you need to cope with your situation in a healthy way and in a way that helps you feel better about yourself and your life.

A survivor of the Nazi death camps, Viktor Frankl, rendered one of his most powerful words on this:

"Everything can be taken from a man but one thing: the last of the human freedoms – to choose one's attitude in any given set of circumstances, to choose one's own way." — **Frankl**

Where Do These Negative Thoughts Come From?

As suggested by Aaron Beck, these thinking patterns are set up in childhood, becoming automatic and relatively fixed. So, for instance, a child who did not experience much open affection from his/her parents but instead, well praised for school work, might start to think, "I must do well all the time. If I don't, I will be rejected." Such a rule for living (which is termed, a **dysfunctional assumption**) may work well for the person most of the time and may even help them work harder. However, if something happens that is out of their control, and they experience setbacks or failure, then the dysfunctional thought pattern could be triggered. This person may then start to have **automatic thoughts** such as, "I have totally failed. No one will like me again. I can't face them."

Cognitive behavioral therapy acts to help the person understand that "this is what is going on." It aims to help him/her step outside their automatic thoughts and test them out. For the depressed woman scenario earlier discussed, CBT would encourage that she examines real-life experiences to see what would happen to her, or to others in a similar situation. Then, in the light of a more realistic perspective, she may be willing to take the chance to test out what other people would think, by revealing her difficulties to friends, families or loved ones.

It should be made clear that negative things can and do happen. But when we are in a distorted state of mind, our predictions and interpretations may be based on a biased view of the situation, thus making it difficult to face them, and even worse, difficult in addressing them from a holistic perspective. CBT helps people to correct these misinterpretations.

The role of a CBT therapist thus is to help you understand and examine your beliefs and help you to make sense of meanings.

CBT as a Doing Therapy

CBT is a great way to understand what keeps a problem going and when armed with the information, our sole job is to take action to get unstuck from the problem. What makes CBT much different is that it is not just a 'talking therapy.' Psychologists have found that for CBT to be really helpful in making changes in your life, it is best to think of it as a 'doing therapy.'

Doing Homework

Working on homework assignments between sessions is a crucial part of the CBT process. However, what this may entail will vary. For instance, at the beginning of the therapy, you might be asked to keep a diary of any incidents that may stir up feelings of anxiety or depression, so that the thoughts surrounding the incident can be examined. You could also be given another assignment later on in the therapy, made up of exercises that will help you cope with problem situations of a specific kind.

Why Do I Need to Do Homework?

People willing to do home assignments get the most benefit from CBT. For instance, most people who suffer from depression say they don't want to take part in work or social activities until they feel better. CBT then introduces them to an alternative viewpoint – that attempting some activity of this nature, albeit small to begin with, will help make them feel better.

Now, if that individual is open to the idea to test this out, he/ she could agree to meet a friend for a drink at the pub. By being open to partaking in a social activity like this, they tend to make faster progress compared to someone who feels unable to take this risk.

Who Can CBT Help?

CBT has been found to be most suitable for people with a particular and identifiable problem that is addressable with specific tasks and goals. CBT's practical nature makes it useful for people looking for a hands-on approach to their treatment. Originally, CBT was developed to be used as a treatment option for depression, but it quickly became adapted to successfully treat people with several health conditions ranging from anxiety to chronic pain and addiction.

CBT as a tool can be used in treating people suffering from mental health problems and other health conditions such as:

- Depression.
- Anxiety (including generalized anxiety disorder, panic attacks, and panic disorder, and social anxiety disorder)
- Post-traumatic stress disorder (PTSD) and dissociative disorders such as depersonalization and derealization

- Obsessive compulsive disorder (OCD)
- Eating disorders including anorexia nervosa and bulimia nervosa
- Personality disorders
- Psychosis and unusual beliefs
- Low self-esteem
- Physical health problems, including chronic pain, and tinnitus
- Medically unexplained symptoms including fatigue and seizures
- Substance and drug use disorders
- Sleep disorders
- Phobias and;
- Sexual disorders

CBT (together with medication) is rapidly generating interest in treating people suffering from hallucinations and delusions, and those with long-term health problems such as irritable bowel syndrome (IBS) and arthritis. Using CBT (a short term therapy) in treating problems that are severely disabling and more long term is less easy to accomplish. Although CBT cannot cure the physical symptoms of these health problems, people can, however, learn its principles to help them cope better with their symptoms, improve their quality of life and increase their chances of making further progress.

CBT Principles – What is CBT Like?

Although therapy must be adapted to suit each person, there are, however, certain principles that underlie cognitive behavior therapy for everyone. Ultimately, CBT aims to teach you to be your own therapist, by helping you understand your current ways of thinking and behaving, and by equipping you with the tools needed to change your maladaptive cognitive and behavioral patterns. Some of the core principles of CBT to guide you along are:

CBT is problem-focused: By remaining focused on the problems you and your therapist identifies, it becomes much easier to produce clear treatment goals and objectives.

CBT emphasizes active participation and collaboration: You and your therapist will work in unison in actively seeking out ways to help with your problem, which may include going into the world to seek other people's input, setting goals, and developing a treatment plan. You may also be required to create your homework assignments. You and your therapist's active participation and collaboration are key during therapy; without it, the goal-oriented and problem-focused approach would be ineffective.

CBT is focused on the present: Since CBT is present-focused such as the feelings of anxiety or depression you feel 'now,' your current problems are therefore discussed. Although there may be some mention of your personal history, past thoughts or behaviors to understand the origin of your problems, beliefs, and interpretations, therapy often occurs with a focus on the here and now of the problems causing you pain and suffering – and this is where you and your therapist have the power to make changes.

CBT sessions are well structured: The structure of sessions will relatively remain constant for the period of treatment. You and the therapist will set a plan and address all the items on the list every week. This approach allows the relationship between you and your therapist to deepen, which is also a core principle of CBT.

CBT is a time-limited approach: CBT sessions are usually short-term, typically between 6 and 20 sessions compared to other forms of therapy that can last for years. This does not imply that CBT treatment is less effective than other forms of therapy – it actually tends to out-perform them.

CBT emphasizes relapse prevention: Learning to stay well is an important part of CBT. By understanding the factors that triggered your anxiety, depression, or any other issues, you can then be able to quickly identify and immobilize warning signs of a relapse when they resurface.

How Effective is CBT?

CBT is an evidence-based form of therapy in which researchers figure out *what* components of therapy is best suited to work, for *which* problems, and *why*. Therapy sessions conducted on an individual basis also pay close attention to evidence: CBT patients are often encouraged to set personal goals (e.g., *"If I were feeling less anxious, do shopping by myself without the need to escape would be a walk in the park for me"*) and then record the data (evidence) about if these goals are being met.

When the question *"how effective is CBT?"* is asked, it means *"what is it effective for?"* and *"effective compared to what?"* There is also a need to examine *"how often the conditions get better by themselves?"*. One way researchers address these questions is by performing what is called randomized controlled trials (RCTs) —where different treatments are systematically and carefully compared to each other. This is the same process applied in medicine to test the effectiveness and safeness of new drugs. In the past few decades, CBT has been examined by thousands of such studies, and researchers can now combine the results of these RCTs to demonstrate in more reliable ways, which treatments are best suited to work. The chart below depicts the result of a meta-analysis of CBT published in 2015. The results were pulled from a total of 48 studies that compared CBT with 'treatment as usual' for close to 7000 people that suffer from anxiety, depression, or mixed anxiety & depression. The results clearly show that CBT is a more favored treatment option, i.e., when compared to their usual treatment, more people become better when they get treated with CBT.

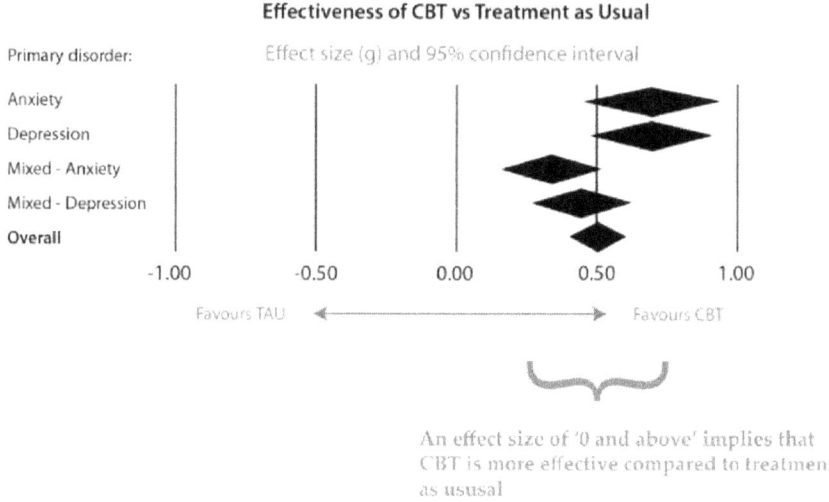

Figure 4: CBT's effectiveness vs. treatment as usual (TAU)

Another way to measure the effectiveness of CBT in treating psychological problems is by taking a look at the 'response rates.' A person is said to 'respond' to therapy if their symptoms have significantly improved by the end of treatment. The chart below depicts the CBT response rates across a wide variety of conditions based on a study of 106 meta-analyses published in 2012.

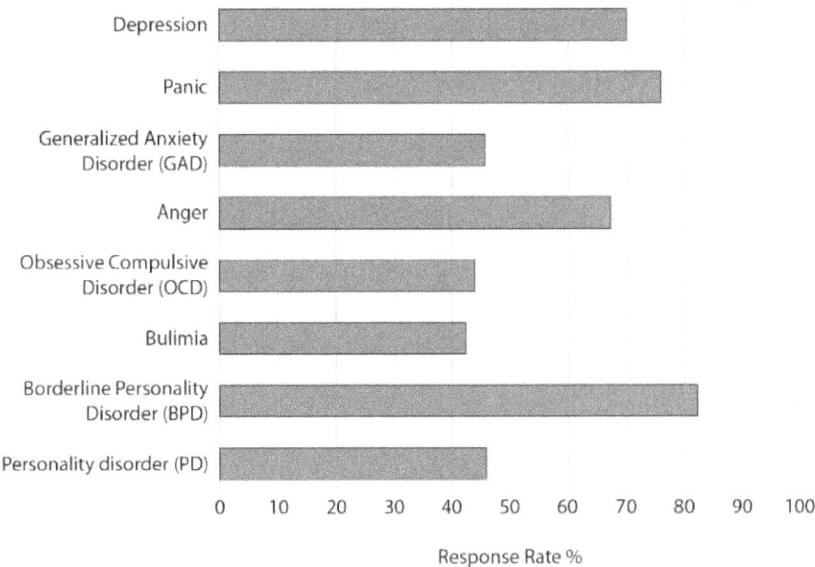

Figure 5: CBT response rates for a variety of conditions (the higher, the better).

I know what you are thinking; "these results are looking good," right? but you may want to ask, *"What do the results look like for the alternatives?"* That same study also compared the CBT response rates to other 'genuine' treatment as usual or forms of therapy. Based on the analysis conducted, it was determined that CBT for depression was as effective as medication or other forms of psychotherapy, but more effective than treatment as usual. CBT for anxiety it was discovered was more effective when compared to other forms of genuine therapies and was credited as a "reliable first-line approach in treating this class of disorders."

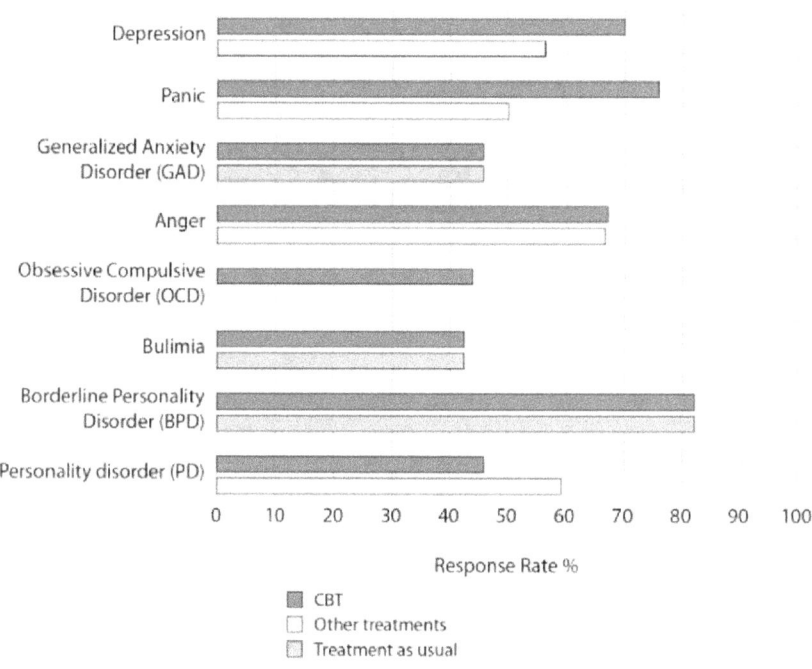

Figure 6: CBT response rates compared to other treatments or treatment as usual.

The overall summary from the reviews, as mentioned above, is that for many conditions, CBT is as effective or more effective when compared to other genuine forms of therapy and better, compared to treatment as usual (which mostly includes check-ups with doctors or use of medications) or doing nothing.

How is CBT Administered?

It is widely recognized that a few patient-therapist face-face sessions of CBT can, for instance, be very helpful in treating people suffering from anxiety and depression. However, not many people can readily have access to a CBT therapist—perhaps there is none within their immediate reach, not covered in their insurance network, or they are costly to afford. It may also be that taking time off from paid work or child care each week to see a therapist can be difficult.

If, for example, you want to try CBT for anxiety or depression and you are unable to see a CBT therapist, take heart, for you may not need to. There are several options through which CBT can be administered without a therapist, which includes self-help books and online-based treatment. Many studies show that self-directed CBT can be very effective.

For example, a review of 33 studies shows that treatment via self-help resulted in significant reductions in anxiety; another review of 34 studies on depression showed similar results, especially when the treatments involved the use of CBT techniques. On average, both reviews found that the self-help treatments were moderately helpful. In other words, people who undertook the self-help treatment felt substantially better—maybe not 100% better, but were noticeably less anxious and depressed.

It is also suggested from these data that people who do self-help CBT for anxiety and depression tend to maintain their progress over a period of time – this shows that people who learn CBT skills on their own can apply the skills to keep feeling better, thus fulfilling one of the major principles of CBT which is to "be your own therapist." Well, I can tell you for a fact that during one of my mental episodes from anxiety and depression, self-help treatments was my regular companion, because although I first had a few in-person therapy sessions with a therapist, it became ultimately expensive to sustain especially as I was out of a job at the time. Overall, I quickly learned to use self-help formats (CBT books and its workbook companion, motivational and inspirational self-help books, etc.), all of which helped me in learning the skills necessary to become my own therapist against anxiety and depression.

But what does this even mean for in-person therapy? Does this mean the end for therapists? Absolutely not. Self-help treatment can likewise be done with limited input from a therapist—for example, a brief phone call every week—which can serve as an extra boost compared to self-help alone. The additional benefit of working with a therapist comes from not only having an expert's input but also having someone who cares and provides constant encouragement.

Although the above statement holds, it should be noted, however, that self-help CBT is most suitable for those with mild to moderate symptoms and generally capable of functioning properly. A severely depressed person who is unable to get out of bed, for instance, is likely not a good match and will most probably need to have a one-on-one treatment with a therapist.

Should you choose to pursue self-help CBT, then:

- Get a book that resonates with you. People are drawn to different methods, level of detail, tones, etc. If you feel the book is a good fit, there is a higher chance you will stay engaged with it.
- Choose a book based on solid research. Self-help therapy takes a considerable amount of time and

effort, so it is advisable to channel your focus toward a program with a solid grounding.

- Create a room in your schedule to go through the program. Therapy of any kind can be tackled at better and worse times. While the likelihood exists that you will always have competing activities, you should avoid times when you are truly overextended to prevent the therapy from being pushed aside or postponed.

- Follow the program as carefully as possible. It is very easy to skip parts of a self-help program that we think would not work, or that we think we already know. One of the dangers of skipping parts of a self-help program is that if you find a program that does not work, you would not know if it is because it was not the right fit for you or because you only did part of it. Following through with the instructions is the best way to benefit and know what actually works for you.

On the flip side, CBT can also be delivered through an online medium in several ways. This can be via a video chat program, e.g., Skype, which is very similar to in-person therapy, with the difference being that both the patient and therapist are miles apart. Computer-based CBT, SMS, Emails, and other online chat media can also be used to administer CBT. Essentially, all these methods use the internet as a means of delivery, which is somewhat similar to what a person may receive with in-person treatment.

A common question about online CBT is if it is as effective as in-person therapy. As earlier mentioned, video chat/ conferencing, for instance, is quite similar to traditional in-person therapy, and it is expected to work equally well. However, a completely automated online CBT treatment, designed by expert clinicians, will almost surely perform way better than in-person treatment program administered by a therapist that is poorly trained. In some ways, I believe the question: "Which is better?" misses the mark.

These systems of CBT treatment does address a critical need in modern mental health treatment. Several people around the world would benefit tremendously from evidence-based techniques such as CBT. However, if for a reason or another, they cannot access in-person services, self-help, and online CBT, including fully automated-computerized CBT, would be their best bet.

The summary of all this is to discover what works best for you, given the peculiarity of your problem, your financial position, insurance coverage as well as your accessibility to in-person therapy.

What Types of CBT Are There?

Certain forms of CBT exercise greater emphasis on the role our thinking plays on feelings and behaviors, while others may focus on the influence of environmental factors. Whichever the case is, the type of CBT that is best suited for you will be determined by the nature of your difficulties, the outcome of previous therapies (if any), your unique background, your preferences, and your unique strengths and weaknesses.

Several types of CBT have been designed over the years. However, I will discuss some of the well-known types of CBT used in the modern world as well as their applications.

- **Cognitive Therapy (CT):** As already mentioned, cognitive therapy was developed by Aaron T. Beck, which was one of the earliest therapies considered as Cognitive Behavior Therapy. Beck hypothesized the Beck Cognitive Triad, which included three types of cognitive distortions that he proposed caused and maintained depressive episodes. These cognitive distortions are about the self, the world, and the future. Take, for instance, a depressed patient who enters therapy with negative thoughts such as, "I am worthless (self)," "people don't seem to like me, and I am bad at doing my job well enough (world)," and things will never change (future)." In particular, negative views about the future can be very problematic because they relate to hopelessness, which in most cases, stands as a risk factor for suicide.

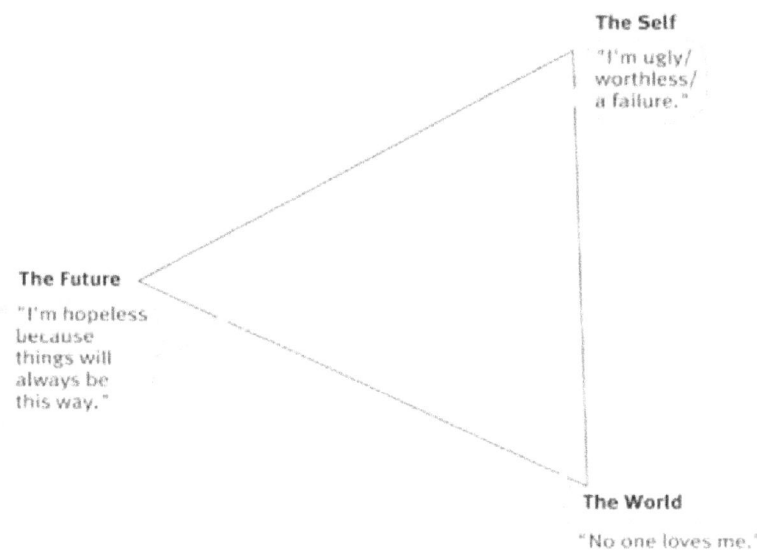

Figure 7

Cognitive therapy was originally designed to treat depression, i.e., major depressive disorder, but has since gained clinical success in reducing anxiety. It is also shown to be an excellent treatment option for people with phobias, generalized anxiety disorder, and ADHD.

Generally speaking, the goal of CT is to spot faulty lines of thinking and reduce irrational thoughts. CT is known for challenging toxic thinking and replacing unhealthy thoughts with more logical and rational ones.

- **Rational Emotive Behavior Therapy (REBT):** Just like Cognitive Therapy, REBT is another earlier form of cognitive behavioral therapy, founded in the 1950s by Albert Ellis that shares some similarities with CT. REBT emphasizes on a patient's irrational beliefs and actively targeting them for a change into more rational ones. To support the use of REBT in treatments, Ellis developed a model called the ABC Technique of Irrational Beliefs. According to this model, Ellis believes the activating event (**A**) is not what causes negative emotional and behavioral consequences (**C**), but instead it is the unrealistic interpretation that a person attributes to the events that result to an irrational belief system (**B**) that helps in causing the consequences (**C**).

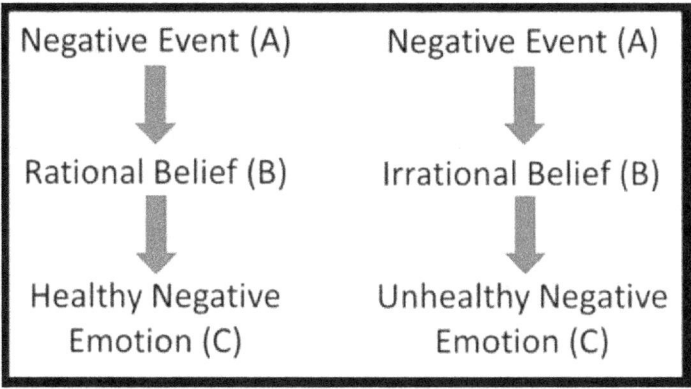

Figure 8

Let's represent the above analogy using an example. Gina is upset because she had bad grades in her math test. The Activating event, A, in this case, is that she had bad grades. Her Belief, B, is that for her not to be seen as worthless, she must have good grades. The Consequence, C, of A and B, is that Gina feels depressed.

Through REBT, Gina, with the help of a therapist, can then identify and confront her irrational beliefs and expectations, e.g., I must be perfect, or I must have good grades to be worthwhile. The therapist would then help Gina to understand that no evidence exists that to be worthwhile, she must have good grades, or that getting bad grades is awful. He would make her see reason that although she desires good grades, which would be good to have, the absence of it, however, would hardly make her worthless.

After confronting Gina's negative thinking by **reframing** it, Gina and the therapist then developed a realistic thinking, which then helped her in developing more rational beliefs and healthy coping strategies. It was only when this was accomplished that Gina was able to change her negative thinking and unrealistic beliefs.

It is this confrontation of Gina's irrational thinking into more rational ones that the ABC model is most often being referred to as the ABCD Model. In this revised model, the D stands for the Disputation of Beliefs. Disputation is not an original member of the ABC Model because it takes place outside of the ABC.

- **Dialectical Behavior Therapy (DBT):** DBT is a behavioral therapy that is also a form of cognitive behavioral therapy. Marsha Linehan originly developed DBT for the treatment of people with the most complex type of syndromes, e.g., borderline personality disorder or impulsive and suicidal behaviors. It is based on a dialectical philosophy that challenges us to confront and make peace with the complex and opposite truths that are often inherent in most situations, the most basic being accepting ourselves or changing ourselves. DBT is a skill-based approach that combines cognitive behavioral techniques with the core skill practice, mindfulness (a non-judgmental, present-centered intentional awareness), and then applying this mindful awareness to life through other major DBT skills such as distress tolerance, interpersonal skills, and emotion regulation. This has proven to shown great results, where other treatments have failed and have since been successfully applied to several problems where dysregulation of emotions and destructive impulsivity interrupted normal living. Mental health disorders where DBT treatment has been applied aside personality problems include eating disorders, depression, and anxiety. It has also been used in treating alcohol and drug abuse as well as explosive anger.

- **Acceptance and Commitment Therapy (ACT):** This form of cognitive behavior therapy for anxiety and other mood-related problems was developed in the 1980s by Steven Hayes, building on ideas from radical behaviorism. Unlike traditional CBT (CBT-interventions based on the idea that our thoughts influence our emotions and behaviors), ACT does not emphasize changing, challenging, or replacing disturbing thoughts, but instead, focuses on the relationship we have with our thoughts by exploring other ways to react differently to how we think. Have you ever noticed that when you are anxious about something, it becomes worsened when you attempt to eradicate the thoughts, engage in over-controlling behaviors or strict, rigid forms of coping? Well, I know this because I experienced it during one of my emotional breakdown episodes. ACT aims to increase psychological flexibility, i.e., the ability to Accept your reactions, to Choose a valued direction, and to Take action (ACT).

  In Acceptance and Commitment Therapy, mindfulness and other ACT exercises are used to break the "living in the past or future" habit and to commit to living in the present moment. Even traditional CBT proposes that anxiety stems from thoughts about the future, while depression is mostly fueled by thoughts focused on the past.

In general, ACT helps us see our old thoughts and ourselves from a different perspective, which then gives us the opportunity to act in new ways around our old thoughts.

- **Cognitive Processing Therapy (CPT):** CPT, developed by psychologist, Patricia Resick, has been shown to treat Post-traumatic Stress Disorder (PTSD) successfully. Military veterans and sexual assault or rape victims form part of the populations of PTSD on which CPT is shown to be an effective form of psychotherapy. Like several forms of CBT, the CPT therapist works to build strong therapeutic rapport, which is especially crucial for PTSD patients that often have safety and trust issues when asked to recall memories about traumatic events. CPT also involves psychoeducation about PTSD; this is to help PTSD patients understand how PTSD symptoms develop and are maintained. During therapy, the patient documents an account of the traumatic experience, and via therapeutic exchanges with the therapist, they become able to identify the specific cognitive distortions present in their belief system. By doing this, they learn how to challenge these cognitive distortions, which, according to theorists, may exacerbate shame, anger, and anxiety, thereby leading to patients avoiding reminders of the traumatic events.

As patients allow more realistic adaptive beliefs, they begin to overtake the cognitive distortions, helping them decrease the behaviors of avoidance, thus leading to reductions both in emotional symptoms and increase in healthy behaviors such as returning to work, a more regular sleep schedule, or increased emotional and physical intimacy, etc. CPT, which combines exposure therapy (a technique used by CBT therapists) as well as cognitive techniques from CBT, has been incorporated by the United States Veteran's Administration into several of their programs to help military veterans who suffer from PTSD.

- **Mindfulness-Based Cognitive Therapy (MBCT):** Developed by psychologists John Teasdale, Zinden Segal, and Mark Williams, MBCT combined the knowledge and techniques of CBT with mindfulness meditation practices. MBCT's most strongest evidence is as a relapse-prevention treatment for people that suffer from depression. That being said, research from scientific studies suggests that MBCT is a very effective form of therapy for people living with high degrees of anxiety, chronic pain, stress, and gastrointestinal problems like IBS (intestinal bowel syndrome). Likewise, it can be very effective in helping people that experience panic attacks, and that includes depersonalization. The goal of MBCT is not to change one's thoughts but changing how a person reacts to his/ her thoughts, thus helping to make healthy choices with each given day and improve life on a moment to moment basis. This type of cognitive approach breaks the spiral of negative toxic thinking, which can worsen emotions such as anxiety and depression.

Pros and Cons of CBT

The approach to CBT does have its advantages and disadvantages. Just like any other therapy, there is always a risk of negative emotion from a traumatic event or experience resurfacing. Let's take a look at what's good and what may hold back progress in treatment, which both the therapist and you, the patient, should be aware of and discuss before or during therapy; Some of which we have already discussed in the preceding pages.

Here is a list of pros:

- One important advantage of cognitive behavioral therapy is that it is designed to be short, ranging from five to ten months when compared to other "talking" therapies.
- CBT can help treat some mental health disorders where it has shown that medication alone has not helped improve symptoms.
- CBT focuses on changing thoughts and behaviors to change how you feel.
- CBT strategies are practical and helpful and can help people in coping with future stresses.
- CBT can help improve emotional processing as well as the quality of life.
- CBT can be provided in several formats such as face-to-face, online, self-help, or even via workbooks. It can likewise be useful in a group setting.
- CBT is useful for all age groups.

Here is a list of cons:

- You have to commit to the process. The therapist has no magic wand to wave that will take away your problems without co-operation.
- CBT emphasizes the capacity of an individual to change their thoughts, feelings, and behaviors and does not address broader problems in families, systems, or environments that could significantly impact their health and wellbeing.
- For people who suffer from severe mental health challenges or with a learning disability, CBT could prove more difficult as a treatment option.
- As CBT addresses the sources of depression, anxiety, or other stress-causing emotions, you may initially feel uncomfortable when exposed to this type of treatment.
- The possible underlying causes of negative emotions are not wholly addressed with the CBT treatment as it emphasizes more on the present problems.
- In real life, while doing the actual work, it could take some time for you to reclaim your mental health and improve your quality of life.

Chapter 2

What Does CBT Involve?

Typically, a patterned, step-wise approach is most times followed when administering CBT. Although the process described herein is linear in fashion, bear in mind that people and the problems they face are not always straightforward, often calling for a 'dance' to and fro between the steps.

Step 1: Identifying the Problem and Setting Goals

During the first few sessions, a CBT therapist wants to uncover the kind of problems troubling you, his patient. This may include issues such as a medical condition, grief, anger, divorce, or symptoms of a mental health disorder. In addition, they will want to explore your goals, i.e., what do you want differently at the end of therapy. To conduct an assessment of your problems, the CBT therapist, will discuss some or all of the following:

- Asking open-ended questions so that you can discuss your problems, e.g., *"Tell me why you are here,"* or *"What has been troubling you of late?"*

- Making a 'problem list' alongside with you and brainstorming together about the relative importance of the individual problems, e.g., *"Now that a list of the things troubling you at the moment has been made, could we try putting the individual problem in the order of how they interfere with the life you desire to lead?"*

- Generating goals that are SMART. Often, this is achieved by focusing on the behaviors you want to change, e.g., *"I want to stop experiencing panic attacks at least three weeks after the end of therapy."* In my book, *How to Stop Overthinking*, I discussed in-depth how you can set effective SMART goals.

- Using structured interviews and questionnaires to determine the presence or absence of symptoms and difficulties, e.g., *"I would ask you a number of questions about your feelings in the past month, and I would like that you answered each question with this five-point scale that goes from 'never' to 'very often'"*

- Asking questions relating to risk, which includes discussing current and past suicidal thoughts and actions, e.g., *"Do you ever have the thoughts of hurting yourself or ending your life?"*

Step 2: Identifying Core Beliefs About the Problems

It is not enough to identify a problem, we also need to find solutions to the problem. In finding solutions to the problem, it is important to understand what keeps the problem going and find some ways to put a stop to it. In understanding what keeps a problem and stopping it, we first need to understand what core beliefs are.

What are Core Beliefs?

Core beliefs are nothing but deep-seated assumptions, underlying ideas, or thoughts you hold about yourself, others, and the world, which over a period of time, you come to believe as true. However, they are mostly developed from our early childhood experiences, which, for most people, does not reflect what is actually true. These beliefs then turn out to impact our feelings, our relationship with others, and our lives in general.

Core beliefs can be positive or negative, but for the examples going forward, we would dwell more on the negative side and how it can be reframed to become positive.

Typically, core beliefs fit into one of the following:

I am _____

People are _____

The world is _____

Below are some examples of negative core beliefs:

- I am ugly and up to no good
- Everyone else does well at their job than I do
- The world is full of greedy and self-centered people

These are all core beliefs. Such inner beliefs dictate our whole lives, which in most cases, are wrong. Negative, and often inaccurate core beliefs like those mentioned above, will drastically lower your chances of experiencing joy and self-fulfillment in life.

How Core Beliefs Develop

Let me describe a clinical example of how core beliefs develop. David's childhood was characterized by how much his parents were very critical and placed great emphasis on academic excellence. His brother excelled academically, but often, he struggled to meet the high standards of his parents. Due to this reason, David developed the core belief, "*I am useless*," and whenever he fails a test, he develops the automatic thought, "*I am a total failure.*"

While core beliefs can be helpful in some cases, most times, they could cause negative emotions. For instance, it has been suggested that people experiencing symptoms of depression are more likely to have core beliefs telling them they are helpless and/ or unloveable. People with anxiety, on the other hand, are more likely to have core beliefs telling them the world is not a safe place. If you suffer from depression, anxiety, or any other conditions, examining your core beliefs would help you and your therapist to understand what keeps your problem up and running and what to do to put an end to it.

In the subsequent sections, I would walk you through how to identify and analyze your core beliefs.

Identifying Core Beliefs

Identifying problematic core beliefs first starts with learning to identify those thoughts that keep bouncing around in your head each day. These thoughts are called *automatic thoughts* simply because they arise and pop into our heads without consciously thinking about them. At this point, you should be aware that core beliefs can lead to automatic negative thoughts

There are two ways you can identify your automatic thoughts. The first is to sit quietly and observe your thoughts. This can be done at any time, but this technique can be found most helpful when you are feeling down and anxious for a while. Note that the idea is not to ponder if these thoughts are right or wrong or true or false but to simply identify the thoughts.

The other way you can identify your automatic thoughts is to recall the times your feelings or emotions shifted abruptly, like when you were angry, anxious, sad, etc. Again, the goal is not to ruminate on the thoughts, we only want to identify them as thoughts, while noting the content. Once these thoughts have been identified, it is very helpful to note them in a thought record. In your thought record, ensure you keep track of:

- The situation, e.g., You did not get the job
- The feelings or emotions you felt, e.g., Anger (at yourself) and Sadness (about not getting the job)
- The automatic thoughts you had, noting them as accurately as possible (This will help you identify distortions in your thoughts vs. facts), e.g., I will always be the second or third choice.

The next step is to use the automatic thoughts noted to drill down to the underlying core beliefs. One of the most powerful techniques used to identify core beliefs is the *downward arrow question and answer technique*. Essentially, this technique aims to ask you questions about your automatic thoughts, which, for every question, has an answer.

By asking questions, therapists can help you to identify your core beliefs through negative automatic thoughts.

A series of negative thoughts will be generated until you reach the core belief.

Here are some sample questions this technique uses:
- What went through your mind then?
- What does this imply to you?
- What do others say about this?

Below is an example of the Downward Arrow Question and Answer Technique in action:

Joe submits his application for a job and receives a call that the position is filled. His first thought is: "I knew it, I did not get the job."

Joe notes this thought when he realizes he is feeling sad and angry several days after the call. So, he questioned himself, "What does this thought imply about me?"

He concludes: "It means I never got the job." And "I will always be the second or third choice."

He then questions himself, "What is the worst thing about not being selected?"

He learns that "It implies I am not good enough."

He then asks, "Why am I so upset about this?"

He concludes that it means "I am not worthy of a good job."

The underlying core belief of Joe is, "I am not worthy."
Joe realizes that he has a strong negative reaction that has gone on for a while. Not only does he feel bad about his core belief, but it could also make him less likely to apply for another position. Therefore, Joe needs to understand the reason for having so much trouble in this situation. Without first identifying his core belief, Joe would be unable to understand nor change it.

One last example:

Jane expresses feelings of helplessness and worthlessness because her daughter has declined to clean her room. Below is an example of the Q & A technique that is applied to Jane's automatic thought to identify her core belief.

Automatic Thought	This room is a mess.
Question:	What does that mean to me?
Answer:	She's a slob!
Question:	Why is that so bad assuming that's true?
Answer:	My friends may see how messy her room is when they come over
Question:	Why is that so bad?
Answer:	They will think I am an inadequate mother
Question:	Why is that so bad assuming that's true?
Answer:	I will feel worthless if my friends disapprove of me = CORE BELIEF!

In general, once you and your therapist have identified problematic core beliefs, your therapist will encourage you to discuss your thoughts about them. This may require that you observe what you tell yourself of an experience (self-talk), interpreting the meaning of a situation, and your beliefs about yourself, others, and the world.

Step 3: Analyzing Core Beliefs by Identifying Cognitive Distortions

In reaching your core belief, you have assumed each answer is true along the way. The key is to recognize that the automatic core beliefs are not necessarily true by asking yourself if they are accurate. If you find negative core beliefs that hold you back, you need to consider where they may have originated from.

Do you hear the voice of a parent from an ugly experience of your childhood?

Are you hearing the echoes of a partner that pulled you down by undermining your self-esteem?

The above are mere examples.

Finding the origins of your core beliefs can help you identify cognitive distortions in each answer provided in each question. This is the first step to changing your core beliefs. Your therapist or counselor can help you with this process if you are really struggling with it. Analyzing your core beliefs is not easy, but doing so can help you root out negative and inaccurate thought patterns. After you have determined the origin of your core beliefs, go through your answers such as that in step 2 above, and look for cognitive distortions.

Note: Depending on the nature of the core beliefs and the circumstances surrounding it, it may be impracticable to associate your core beliefs with an origin. In such a case, simply look for cognitive distortions from each answer provided.

What are Cognitive Distortions?

Cognitive distortions or unhelpful thinking styles are inaccurate ways of thinking, which may seem true, accurate, or real.

Sometimes, our brains take 'short cuts' in generating results that are not entirely accurate. Different cognitive short cuts lead to several kinds of bias or distortions in how we think. Sometimes we jump to the worst conclusion possible, while at other times, we hold ourselves responsible for things that are not our fault. Cognitive distortions are prevalent amongst everyone, automatic, completely normal, and not our fault. A study suggests that people develop cognitive distortions as a survival method in coping with adverse life events. Unless we learn to identify them when they arise and contain them, the effects it could have on our moods and lives can be very powerful. By understanding the different types of cognitive distortions, you are on the way to spotting the thinking traps that hold you back.

Types of Cognitive Distortions

To help you get started in spotting your cognitive distortions, below are some of the key thought habits generally known to cause distress, which also includes anxiety and depression. You can take a cue from the examples to spot your cognitive distortions:

Jumping to conclusions: It is when you predict the outcome of a situation will turn out badly without holistically looking at all the possible scenarios.

E.g., He did not call me; he wants to break up with me.

Blaming: You play the victim mentality by blaming others or yourself for the problems in your life while giving up control of your feelings.

E.g., He makes me so miserable!

All or Nothing Thinking: You see things in black or white terms, with no shades of gray. If you make a mistake, you see yourself as a failure.

E.g., I am a bad mother

Disqualifying the Positive: In a given situation, instead of just ignoring the positive aspects or filtering it out, you further dismiss it as a fluke, argue against it, or focus on the negative.

E.g., Although she asked that I mentor a coworker due to my competence, she has no idea that I really do not know a lot

Emotional Reasoning: You lose objectivity of the facts by sticking to the interpretations of yourself based on your emotions and negative self-image.

E.g., I feel like a stupid person, so I must be a stupid person.

Fallacy of Fairness: You expect life to be fair.

E.g., I should get what I deserve because life should be fair.

Fortune Telling: Your prediction of the future outcome is negative due to your distorted way of thinking. You think you know the end game of what will happen without any factual evidence.

E.g., I will never love again.

Overgeneralization: You draw a general conclusion about your ability, performance, or self-worth on the basis of a single incident.

E.g., Nobody likes me

Labeling and Mislabeling: You label others or yourself using terms such as lazy, stupid, loser, fat, jerk, by stating them as though they are facts. This is an extreme form of overgeneralization.

E.g., I am just so fat and lazy, and he is a jerk.

Magnification or Minimization: Things are either blown out of proportion, or you deny something is a problem when it actually is.

E.g., It is not a big deal (when it really is to you) and,
      It is AWFUL that he said that!

Mental Filter: You single out a negative aspect in a given situation and dwelling exclusively on it, thereby perceiving the whole situation as negative.

E.g., My big nose makes me look so unattractive.

Personalization: Your think things are about you, and when you do, your interpretations are distorted, i.e., If someone is negative or angry, you take responsibility for such things that are outside your control even when there is no basis for doing so.

E.g., My child is depressed, and it is my fault.

Should Statements: A pre-condition on how you and others "should" be such as having judgmental and unforgiving expectations that use "musts" and "shoulds."

E.g., I should not be so angry about this." "He should know this already!"

Can you relate to any of the above examples? Does any of them look familiar to you? Can you spot an underlying trend of distorted thinking patterns that may be contributing to your problem?

Using the examples above, I urge you to go on to identify your cognitive distortion. If you are going through the process of identifying your distorted thoughts with a therapist, you may be asked to pay attention to your physical, emotional, and behavioral responses in different situations.

Steps to Identifying Cognitive Distortions

If you want to identify cognitive distortions in your negative automatic thoughts due to your emotions or feelings from a given situation, ensure to do the following:

- Name the feeling, e.g., Ask yourself, "What am I feeling? And respond, "I am feeling anxious and sad."

- Validate the feeling, e.g., Put your hand over your heart and say "anxious," "sad," and breathe into the feeling of being anxious and sad. Observe where you felt these feelings in your body, focus on that part of your body, and send warm breath to it like you would a child who feels sad.

- Find the thoughts (cognitive distortions) under the feeling by asking yourself:

    "What are the thoughts that trigger these feelings?"

    E.g., Last night, I was at a work party where I drank too much. When I talked to people at the party, I think I made a fool of myself, and probably said or did something I should not have. Everyone now thinks I am completely screwed up. I would have no more friends, and my boss will fire me; I cannot show up at work tomorrow. I am so mortified that I feel like disappearing. I am such a fat pig.

Some of the thoughts are, "I made a fool of myself, and everyone thinks I am completely screwed up, no one will want to be my friend, I am getting fired, I am a fat pig." These are examples of cognitive distortions. Let's see why below.

- Name the cognitive distortion:

    Should Statements: I should never look out of control.

    Jumping to Conclusions: No one will want to be my friend. I am getting fired.

    Labeling and Mislabeling: I am a fat pig

Step 4: Cognitive Restructuring or Challenging Your Negative Automatic Thoughts

Cognitive restructuring or challenging negative automatic thoughts is a mainstay of CBT. It describes the process by which people are trained to change how they think by the examination of their thoughts for bias or inaccuracy and replacing them with more balanced thoughts.

After identifying your cognitive distortions, your therapist will encourage you to question yourself on if your perspective of a situation is based on facts or on an inaccurate view of what is going on. This will help you to challenge them by responding reasonably at each step.

A number of CBT techniques are available in challenging negative thoughts and responding reasonably to them. I will, however, discuss some of the most common ones below:

- Traditional disputation. This method involves the examination of the evidence for and against a thought. People often find reasons why a thought is true but may need assistance in considering why a particular thought may not be 100% true at all times. Once evidence for and against an automatic thought has been generated, either you or at the behest of your therapist would be required to write a balanced thought, taking into account all of the evidence generated.

- Court-trial style disputation. Some people find it helpful when they view the disputation process using the court-trial style. In this method, you will function as the defense attorney, prosecutor, jury, and judge all at once. The automatic thought is placed 'in the dock,' and as the defense attorney, you will argue why the thought is true, and as the prosecutor, why it is false. As the jury, you weigh the evidence, and as the judge, you read the verdict, taking into account all of the evidence.

- Compassionate cognitive restructuring. This method examines the negative thought through a compassionate lens by considering the compassionate perspective of what you would say to others in a similar situation as well as what a compassionate person would say to you.

Finding the Objective Truth About the Thoughts

Using the technique above and the example cited under *Steps to Identifying Cognitive Distortions*, I will demonstrate how to challenge your thoughts and respond rationally.

- What is absolutely true for the cognitive distortions identified?

    What is absolutely true is that I drank a lot and that I am mortified and feel like disappearing.

- How do you know this is true?

    Because I said things I would not have said if I was not drinking.

- Are there any thoughts here that might be untrue?

    It might be untrue I made a fool out of myself. It might be untrue I did or said something I should not have. It might be untrue everyone thinks I screwed up. It might be untrue I would not have any more friends.

- How do you know these thoughts might be untrue?

  Because I am not a mind reader, and I cannot decipher what everyone thinks.

- What is the more balanced truth here?

  The truth is that I am not the first person to have gotten drunk at an office party. As a matter of fact, many people were drinking, and some drank a lot. I doubt many people noticed what I said or did. In functions like this, most people are usually very anxious about what others think of them that I imagine only a few people waste their time obsessing over what I did or did not say. Besides, if one night of being drunk makes me lose my friends, I will know they were not real friends anyway.

You can then go ahead to respond reasonably to each type of <u>cognitive distortions we identified</u>. Using the sample questions and answers from step 2, *<u>Identifying Core Beliefs About the Problems</u>*, let's now also respond reasonably to the distortions in thoughts (assuming you have already applied the techniques above to find the objective truth as already demonstrated).

Initial Responses (Automatic Thoughts)	Reasonable Responses
She's a slob!	To be frank, she's very neat in areas that are important to her, such as her looks.
My friends may see how messy her room is when they come over	Even if they do, several mothers have daughters whose room might be sloppy but yet worthwhile.
They will think I am an inadequate mother	They might just think I am as fallible as they are.
I will feel worthless if my friends disapprove of me = CORE BELIEF!	I don't have to be perfect or have the approval of anyone to be happy and to feel worthwhile. Since no one is perfect, I would rather decide to feel worthwhile for myself.

Going through the process above will help you become rational in reframing not only your negative automatic thoughts but also your negative core beliefs.

Making the Restructured Thoughts Habitual

It is often helpful when you overlearn the habit of identifying automatic thoughts and restructuring your automatic negative thinking. Once you have sufficiently practiced the art of journaling your thoughts using a thought record, it is worthwhile to go through the disputation practice in your head. Your therapist can help you through this process as you do so. Many people often report that doing this soon becomes second-nature to them in noticing automatic thoughts when they pop up – prompting them to ask, among others, "What is the evidence to believe this thought is true?".

An example;

After therapy, Joan learned to monitor her actions and emotional responses. She began by planning the activities that gave her a boost in dealing with the situations she had avoided through fear. She learned to identify when she was biased or extreme in her thinking and became very skilled at analyzing her emotion-driven thoughts by reasoning them out to get things into the right perspective. Her mood after that, noticeably improved, and she was able to tackle long-standing problems.

Step 5: Monitor Your Feelings

Cognitive behavioral therapy places great emphasis on monitoring problems and symptoms. Just like thoughts can be biased, our impressions about the effectiveness of therapy can also be biased. You and/or your therapist can overcome this bias by often measuring the symptoms and problems about whether the therapy is going in the right direction. Regularly monitoring outcomes can help achieve better results.

Symptom monitoring can be as simple as checking in with the feeling again and asking, how are you feeling now?

Still anxious, but a bit relaxed. For now, I can get up and walk away from this. I don't have to stuff something down my mouth to feel better. I can breathe through it, knowing that several of my feelings of anger, guilt, sadness, and shame are not the objective truth, but rather, just self-imposed thoughts.

Symptom monitoring can also mean counting how often something happens, such as counting how often a person with panic experiences panic attacks, or counting how often a person with OCD exhibits one of their compulsions. For anxiety and depression, specific measures might be used to explore the kinds of thoughts experienced by someone.

John came to therapy because he experiences panic attacks. At the beginning of therapy, he was asked by his therapist to keep a record of how many panic attacks he experiences every week. Then each week, they would check for updates on what was happening. Upon completion of treatment, John was pleased not to have experienced any panic attacks in the previous three weeks.

Ultimately, monitoring your feelings, symptoms, or problems aims to check if the goal(s) set in step 1 has been met.

The steps involved in CBT, as discussed above, are the generally accepted method of administering CBT to anyone with a mental or health condition. That being said, conditions such as anxiety and depression, among others, require other specific techniques to be employed as complementary efforts to these steps. The next section of this book would focus on how to use other specific CBT techniques against anxiety, depression, anger, and panic attacks.

See you on the other side!

Exercise

- Based on our discussions in this chapter, use the thought record below to identify your problem situation/ trigger (depression, anxiety, anger or panic attacks related), the emotions or feelings you experienced from the situation, the distorted/ irrational thoughts you had about the situation, the evidence against the distorted thoughts, and your restructured, realistic and more balanced thoughts.

Situation / Trigger	Feelings Emotions – (Rate 0 – 100%) Body sensations	Distorted/ Unhelpful Thoughts / Images	Facts providing evidence against the unhelpful thoughts	Restructured and more balanced, realistic thoughts.	Outcome Re-rate emotion
What happened? Where? When? Who with? How?	What emotion did you feel at the time? What else? How intense was it? What did you notice in your body? Where did you feel it?	What went through your mind? What disturbed you? What did those thoughts/ images mean to you, or say about you or the situation? What are you responding to? What would the worst thing about that be, or that could happen?	What facts do you have to validate that the unhelpful thoughts are not true? Is it possible that this is an opinion and not a fact? What did others say about this?	STOP!! Take a breath... What would someone else say about this situation? Is there a bigger picture? Is there some other way of seeing it? What advice would you give someone else in a similar situation? Is my reaction proportional to the actual event? Is this really as important as it seems?	What are you feeling now? (0-100%) What else can you do differently that could be more effective? What will be the consequences? What will be most helpful for you or the situation?

A Short message from the Author:

Hey, I hope you are enjoying the book? I would love to hear your thoughts!

Many readers do not know how hard reviews are to come by and how much they help an author.

I would be incredibly grateful if you could take just 60 seconds to write a short review on the product page of this book, even if it is a few sentences!

Thanks for the time taken to share your thoughts!

Your review will genuinely make a difference for me and help gain exposure for my work.

Section II

Cognitive Behavioral Therapy Strategies

Chapter 3

CBT for Depression

Understanding Depression

Depression is a low mood that can last for a significant amount of time. The severity of depression varies from a mild depression – which might not prevent you from carrying out your normal activities or seeking enjoyment in life, even though it might be difficult to do, to more severe depression – which can leave you unable to function normally and with feelings of suicide and death. The major component of depression is that the pervasive feeling of sadness continues for weeks or months on end, and not just a passing 'blue mood' for a day or two. Depression (commonly called clinical depression or major depressive disorder) is a feeling that is often accompanied by lack of energy (or feeling "weighed down"), a sense of hopelessness, and having little or no interest in the things that once gave joy and happiness.

Major Depressive Disorder is the leading cause of disability in the US (among ages 15-44), according to the National Institute of Mental Health (NIMH), and it is estimated that about 6.7% of the adult population in the US is affected by Major Depressive Disorder in a given year. According to NIMH (2019), risk factors associated with depression ranges from a family history of mood disorders to trauma, major life changes, other physical diseases (e.g., cancer), or even certain prescription medications.

Symptoms of Depression

As already mentioned, depression does not end after just a day or two — it will continue for weeks on end, causing interference with the person's school, work their relationship with others, as well as their ability to enjoy life and have fun.

The symptoms of depression include most of the signs highlighted below, and are experienced nearly every day over two or more weeks:

- a continuous feeling of sadness or loneliness
- lack of energy or feeling weighed down
- feelings of hopelessness

- sleeping difficulties (too much or too little)
- eating difficulties (too much or too little)
- difficulties with concentration or attention
- complete loss of interest in socializing or fun activities
- feelings of worthlessness and guilt
- and/or thoughts of suicide or death

It should interest you to know that most people who feel depressed do not experience every symptom mentioned above, and the presentation of symptoms also differs in degree and intensity from person to person.

Causes & Diagnosis

Ever wondered what causes depression? Perhaps you have been diagnosed with a major depressive disorder, and that has led you to question why some get depressed, and others don't.

Depression does not discriminate against who it can affect, not by age, race, gender, relationship status, or if a person is rich or poor. Anyone can be affected by depression at any point in their life, and that includes children and adolescents (although sometimes, it is seen more as irritability than a sad mood in teens and children).

No single factor is identified to be responsible for this condition. A combination of factors is likely the cause. For some, there are clear triggers, while for others, it can be difficult to understand why they are depressed. Irrespective of which it is, depression can be a result of genetics, gut bacteria, personality, neurobiological makeup, family history, and psychological, environmental, and social factors. Other factors that may increase the possibility of depression are:

- certain medications
- **critical incidents,** e.g., losses (death of a loved one, end of a relationship, job loss), transitions (retiring, having a baby), or financial problems
- abuse
- serious illness
- substance abuse and;
- the tendency to think negatively

CBT Treatment for Depression

Can depression be successfully treated? Yes, fortunately, **depression is a treatable disorder**. According to NIMH and several research studies conducted over the past six decades, clinical depression can readily be treated with short-term, goal-oriented psychotherapy and modern antidepressant medications. For some people, depending on the severity of their condition, a combination of both would work best. Psychotherapy, which has been scientifically proven to work with depression is one of the most laudable treatments for all types of depression, and the approach it uses include cognitive behavioral therapy, psychodynamic therapy, and interpersonal therapy (Gelenberg et al., 2010). Amongst these approaches, CBT is the most widely recognized and generally accepted method being practiced in the modern world.

When it comes to CBT, several techniques, tools, and interventions are available at your disposal. Some of these techniques are best-suited in a therapist-patient setting, while for others, they lend themselves quite well to an individual or 'self-help' situation.

CBT techniques can likewise be used in tandem or individually. It all depends on the setting, the issue, or the circumstance, as well as the person seeking help. That is one cool thing with CBT techniques – there is no one-size-fits-all, or 'cookie-cutter' way to use them.

The techniques I am going to discuss here all have one thing in common – they are built upon the foundations of CBT, which is identifying maladaptive thinking and making intentional, specific, and strategic behavioral changes to achieve the desired result. There are general CBT techniques (like that discussed in Chapter 2, which is the golden standard for all types of conditions), while others are more targeted to specific needs or issues, and these techniques that are more targeted to certain needs (e.g., someone suffering from depression) would be my focus in the following sections.

Before we deep dive into these specific techniques you can start applying right away, it is essential we first discuss some key concepts to give you a solid research-based perspective on how depression works.

What Keeps Depression Going?

Cognitive behavioral therapy is always very interested in figuring out what keeps a problem going. The reason for this is because if we can figure out what keeps a problem going, then we can treat it by distorting its maintenance cycle. To understand what keeps depression going, CBT therapists and researchers proposed two major theories:

- Behavioral model
- Cognitive model

If you have religiously followed the pages of this book, by now, you would have realized that we have virtually touched on all the models above. However, I want to take a different approach to briefly explain these models as it pertains to depression.

Behavioral Theory of Depression

The behavioral theory of depression notes the presence of a strong relationship between the things you do and how you feel. Take, for instance, when you feel good, you are more than likely to partake in activities you enjoy, spend time with people who make you happy, and take on new tasks and adventures that are challenging to you as a person.

The reverse is likewise true, which is you are more than likely to do less when you are depressed, and so, you are left with fewer opportunities to feel pleasure from the activities you enjoy, take on new tasks, and spend time friends and loved ones – the things you need to feel good. This makes it easy to fall into the trap of:

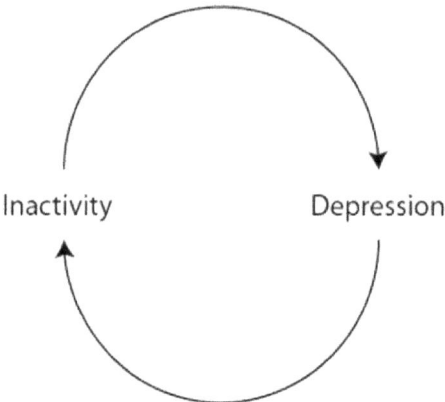

Figure 9: The behavioral model postulates that a lack of rewarding activity results in depression, which then results in further inactivity.

When you are depressed, your motivation works in reverse – you will need to become pleasurably active before you can feel good again. One very effective way of breaking the vicious cycle of depression is to increase your level of pleasant activity *even if you do not feel like it*. This behavioral technique is called Behavioral Activation (BA) or Pleasant Activity Scheduling (PAS), an evidence-based treatment for depression – to be discussed in detail shortly.

Cognitive Theory of Depression

According to the cognitive model, depression is underpinned by negatively biased thinking patterns, i.e., *how you think affects how you feel*. For instance, when you are happy, your thoughts become optimistic, and you can see the bright side of things even when stressful situations occur. But when depressed, your thoughts can become very extreme and very negative, which often makes you interpret situations in negative ways that make you feel bad. Depressing thoughts can be about one's self, the world or other people, and one's future.

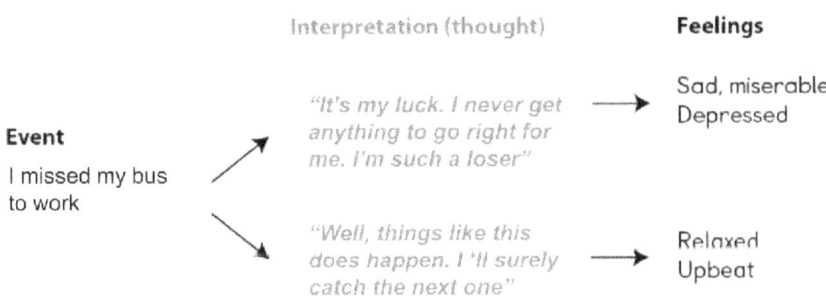

Figure 10: How you interpret events or situations determines how you feel about them.

A cognitive or CBT therapist can help you in identifying unhelpful ways in which you think and will help you in practicing several ways of thinking – one of which might be helping you interpret things in a more balanced way. Two very important techniques used in achieving this are called, Identifying Cognitive Distortions and Cognitive Restructuring. You would agree with me that we discussed extensively on these techniques in [Chapter 2](), so there won't be a need to revisit them. I advise that you go through [Chapter 2]() if you are yet to. Another well known cognitive treatment technique for depression, especially in preventing relapse is Mindfulness-Based Cognitive Therapy (MBCT).

CBT Technique for Depression

By the end of this section, I would have discussed four important techniques you can apply right away to overcome depression instantly; the third technique is our next focus.

Behavioral Activation

Behavioral activation (BA), or Pleasant Activity Scheduling is all about making your life pleasurable and meaningful again. A proactive way to break the vicious cycle of depression is to increase your level of activity even if you do not feel like it. To perform behavioral activation effectively, you need to adhere to the following steps:

- Activity monitoring – recording what you do and how you feel daily.
- Reviewing your "activity monitoring" to understand the relationships existing between your activity and your mood.
- Identifying your values to work out what matters to you in life.
- Scheduling and executing worthwhile activities to boost your experiences of pleasure and achievement.
- Solving any problems or barriers to activation – to ensure you stay on course.

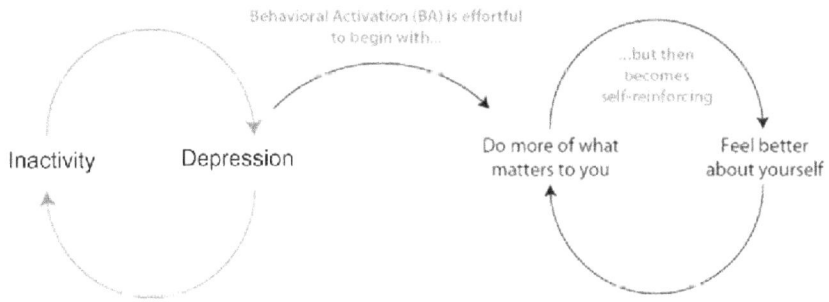

Figure 11

I will walk you through each step highlighted above to get you started with behavioral activation.

Step 1: Activity monitoring

Activity monitoring is the first step in behavioral activation therapy, which aims to monitor your activity and mood for a better understanding of how your depression works.

An activity monitoring worksheet can be used to record what you do for every hour of the day and for a week. Ensure you record everything on this worksheet, even the activities that do not seem important to you. Also, for each time slot, rate your mood on a scale of 1 to 5 – 1 represents feeling very depressed, and 5 represents feeling very good. The goal is to work out how your mood changes as you undertake different activities.

	Monday	Tuesday	Wednesday	Sunday	Mood
06:00 – 07:00	Sleeping	Went Shopping	Facebook	Watched Tv	2
07:00 – 08:00					
08:00 – 09:00					
09:00 – 10:00					
10:00 – 11:00					
11:00 – 12:00					
12:00 – 13:00					

Key

Mood

1 = Very Depressed
2 = Mildly Depressed
3 = Neutral
4 = Fairly Good
5 = Very Good

Exercise 1

1. Using the template above, make a note of every activity you do for each hour of the day for 7 days a week. This can be recorded in a journal or on a note-taking app on your phone.

Step 2: Review your activity monitoring

After monitoring your activity for a week, use your activity monitoring record to spot patterns between your activity and your mood. Look at your completed activity monitoring worksheet and ask yourself the following questions:

- Which activities are associated with your highest mood? When your mood was highest, what were you doing?
- Which activities are associated with your lowest mood? When your mood was lowest, what were you doing?
- What did you observe about the relationship that existed between your mood and how active you were?
- Were there days you did not leave the house? On those days, what was your mood like?
- On the days you were most active, what was your mood like?

Exercise 2

1. Upon answering the questions above, make a list of the activities that made you feel good, and made you feel bad. This list will be used in step 4.

Activities That Made Me Feel Good	Activities That Made Me Feel Bad
1	1
2	2

Step 3: Identify your values

Our values are a reflection of what we hold dear in life. They are what you deeply care about and consider to be important. Our values also reflect how we engage with ourselves, with the those around us, and with the world. Values differ from goals in that goals are achievable. For example, you might hold the value of *being a good parent* very dear to you, which may require an effort of a lifetime, while having a specific goal of *getting your children to school on time*.

Below are examples of values held dear by some people. There might be values you feel that are essential, and others that do not mean much to you. There are no right or wrong answers. Using the descriptions below, think of what makes a meaningful life that you could value.

Value	Description
Family	What kind of relationship do you wish to have with your family? What type of /father / brother / mother /sister/ uncle/ aunt / nephew/ niece/ do you wish to be? How do you wish to be in these relationships?
Marriage / couple / intimacy	What kind of husband/wife/partner do you wish to be? What type of relationship do you wish to be a part of? What type of partnership do you wish to build? What kind of person do you wish to be in a relationship?
Parenting	What type of parent do you wish to be? What qualities do you wish your children see in you? What kind of relationship do you wish to build with your children?
Friendships / social life	What type of friend do you wish to be? What type of friendships is important for you to cultivate? How would you prefer to behave toward your friends? What kind of social life is important to you?
Career /	What kind of work do you find

employment	valuable to you? What are the qualities you wish to bring as an employee? What kind of work relationships would you rather build?
Education / personal growth / development	How would you want to grow as a person? What kind of skills would you want to develop? What matters to you about education and learning? What would you like to know more about?
Recreation/ fun / leisure	How would you like to enjoy yourself? What relaxes you? When are you most playful?
Spirituality	What kind of relationship do you want with God/nature / the Earth?
Citizenship / environment / community	What kind of environment do you want to be a part of? How do you want to contribute to your community? What kind of citizen would you like to be?
Health / physical wellbeing	What kind of values do you have regarding your physical wellbeing? How important to you is your health? How do you want to look after yourself?

Exercise 3

1. Using the examples provided above, take some time thinking about your values – which do you find important to you? How successful have you lived your life in the past month per your values? Use the table below to guide your thought process as you document your response in your journal and feel free to add more values not captured in the table.

Value	Description of your values	Importance How important is this value to you? (Rate 1-5)	Success How successful have you lived per this value in the past month? (Rate 1–5)
Family			
Marriage / couple / intimacy			
Parenting			
Friendships / social life			

Career / employment			
Education / personal growth / development			
Recreation / fun / leisure			
Spirituality			
Citizenship / environment / community			

Key

Importance	Success
1 = Not Important	1 = Not Successful
2 = Least Important	2 = Least Successful
3 = Neutral	3 = Neutral
4 = Fairly Important	4 = Fairly Successful
5 = Very Important	5 = Very Successful

Step 4: Scheduling and executing worthwhile activities

The next step of behavioral activation is to become active. By now, you know it is important to increase your activity level even if you do not feel like it. To kick-start the planning of your activity and sticking to it, write down a selection of likely activities in your journal.

Great places to get some activation targets for your activity plan are:

- **From your activity monitoring exercise:** Which activities worked best at improving your mood from step 2 exercise?
- **From your values assessment exercise:** Which values matter most to you? What activities could you do that may line up with your values? If for example, family is one of the things you value most, perhaps as an activity, you could plan to spend quality time with them.
- **Ensure you do the basics:** Be sure to include targets such as daily brushing of your teeth, doing laundry weekly, cooking meals, shopping, and some socializing activities.
- **Use an activity menu:** Using a list of the activities that helped other people, pick some you think would lift your mood. You can take a cue from the sample activity menu below.

> **Activity Menu**
> Do some exercise
> Meet a friend for coffee
> Cook a meal for someone
> Clean the house
> Take a bath
> Listen to music you like
> Do something nice for someone

Exercise 4

1. After writing down a selected list of possible activities, it is time to create an activity hierarchy. This will help you select the best activities to start with. To create your activity hierarchy, write down the list of the possible activities, and rank them per how difficult you feel they will be to accomplish (1 = not difficult, 5 = very difficult).

   See sample below

Activity	Difficulty (Rate 1-5)
Go to an exercise class once this week	5
Get out of bed by 8 am every day	4
Go for a haircut	3
Repair the kitchen shelf	2

2. Schedule by writing down some activities for the next week by selecting some activities that have low difficulty ratings. It is important that you are specific about:

- **What** the activity is
- **When** you will do it
- **Where** you will do it
- **Who** you might do it with

See sample below

Activity (What?)	Details (When? Where? Who?)	Outcome & Rate Mood (Rate mood 1-5)
Go to an exercise class	Tuesday at 6 pm	Completed - 5
Get out of bed	By 8 am every day	5 out of 7 days - 2
Go for a haircut	Thursday lunchtime, barber near home	Completed - 4
Repair the kitchen shelf	Monday morning, at home	Completed - 3

Key

Mood

1 = Very Depressed
2 = Mildly Depressed
3 = Neutral
4 = Fairly Good
5 = Very Good

After planning the activities in advance for a week, the next step is to put them into action. Good luck!

Step 5: Solving any problems or barriers to activation

- **Do not start too hard:** Life is not a sprint but a marathon. Overall, your activity level has to be greater than your depression level; however, it has to be realistically achievable.
- **Break down activities into smaller steps:** Let's assume you identified the value of being independent, but you are living with your parents. Some helpful steps you can take toward your value might be doing some financial budgeting and planning to work out a move into your own place.
- **Reward yourself:** Make the effort in acknowledging when you completed an activity and not just rushing onto the next target. Some people use a 'check off' for activities that have been completed as an acknowledgment that it has been done. What would a fair reward be if all activities were completed? Think of a way you can treat yourself if you completed half or all of your planned activities.

- **Always remind yourself why you are doing this:** Thoughts like *"when I feel better I'll do it"* are insidious, and depression through this can creep back in. Ofter remind yourself that it is important to be active *even if you do not feel like it* and that one of the most effective treatments for depression is through behavioral activation.

Mindfulness

Mindfulness-based cognitive therapy (MBCT) is a type of therapy birthed from the union of cognitive therapy and meditative principles. The marriage of these ideas resulted in a potent therapeutic tool **used by therapists in helping people experience a unique kind of relationship with their thoughts and minds.**

Two experiments conducted to test the effectiveness of MBCT on depression showed that the relapse rates for this disorder decreased (Teasdale et al., 2000; Kuyken et al., 2008), while a more recent study in patients from several age groups demonstrated the applicability of MBCT in treating different illnesses such as depression, and anxiety (Haydicky, Carly, Wiener, & Ducharme, 2015; Kishita, Takei, & Stewart, 2016; Schroevers,

Tovote, Snippe, & Fleer, 2016). Although mindfulness is widely used, one area MBCT is thought to have strong evidence in its effectiveness is in the treatment of people who have experienced three or more depressive episodes – thus helpful, especially to prevent relapse in depression (Mental Health Foundation).

There are lots of mindfulness techniques and techniques that can help you cope with mental illness such as depression, and they can be practiced with or without the guidance of a therapist. Some of these techniques include:

- Mindful Meditation
- Mindful Observation
- Mindful Listening
- Mindful Breathing
- Mindful Walking
- Guided Meditation
- Self-Compassion Break and;
- Body Scan

In my book, *How to Stop Overthinking*, I discussed extensively on each of these techniques and how they can be practised effectively.

Vagus Nerve Stimulation Therapy

As you explore your depression during therapy or self-administration, you may also want complementary therapies designed to bring down your overall depression levels and help you achieve emotional balance. One such therapy that has gained wide acceptance and now being practised in the treatment of depression is called **Vagus Nerve Stimulation,** a nerve that wanders from your brain into your body, i.e., from your brainstem linking your neck, thorax (chest), and abdomen (belly).

In this unique treatment approach, a vagus nerve stimulation device is used, which is **administered by gently pressing the device against your neck to stimulate the vagus nerve by sending pulses of electrical signals to this nerve.** The vagus nerve is targeted because of its ability to modulate depression, and it has been demonstrated to be highly effective in treatment-resistant depression.

Other vagus nerve stimulation practices are likewise used as a treatment option for depression. Such practices include:

- Deep and slow breathing
- Sudarshan Kriya Yoga, and;
- Auricular Acupuncture among others

In his book, *The Secrets of Vagus Nerve Stimulation*, Dr. Lee Henton demystifies the complexities of the vagus nerve in the treatment of depression and other conditions such as anxiety. If you are interested in reading further on the subject of Vagus Nerve Stimulation as an alternative/ complementary therapy for depression, then click this link or use this web address https://amzn.to/2Kp4PAK.

Chapter 4

CBT for Anxiety

Understanding Anxiety, Worry, and Fear

According to the National Institute of Mental Health (NIMH), about 19% of US adults and 31% of adolescents (ages 13 to 18) experience anxiety every year. Anxiety is an umbrella term that describes feelings of worry, fear, nervousness, or apprehensiveness – these are all part of our everyday lives. We all get anxious about something at some point in our lives, but simply experiencing the feelings of anxiety does not mean you need to seek professional help or that you suffer from an anxiety disorder. In fact, anxiety is an essential and sometimes helpful warning signal against a dangerous or difficult situation. Without anxiety, we would be unable to anticipate dangers and difficulties and prepare for them. Anxiety becomes a disorder when the symptoms become chronic that it occurs quite too often, goes on for a long time, and interferes with your daily activities and ability to function properly.

Anxiety disorders fall into a set of distinct diagnoses, which is dependent on the severity and symptoms of the anxiety being experienced by a person. Different types of unhealthy thoughts are also associated with different types of anxiety disorder. These disorders include:

- Panic disorder/ Panic Attacks
- Obsessive-compulsive disorder (OCD)/ Intrusive Thoughts
- Phobias (e.g., Agoraphobia, Specific/Simple Phobia, and Social Phobia/Anxiety)
- Generalized anxiety disorder (GAD)
- Social anxiety disorder (SAD)
- Post-traumatic stress disorder (PTSD)

Irrespective of the specific disorder, they often follow a similar pattern, i.e., people who suffer from anxiety tend to react more extremely to unpleasant/ unhelpful thoughts, feelings, and situations and may try managing their reactions by **avoiding triggers**. Sadly, such avoidance behavior only serves to reinforce fears and worries. To manage anxiety, most modern types of therapy tend to address this negative thinking and avoidance behavior.

Symptoms of Anxiety

At some point in time of our lives, we have experienced fleeting symptoms associated with anxiety. Such feelings — such as your heart pounding for no apparent reason, having shortness of breath, experiencing tunnel vision, or dizziness usually pass by as quickly as they come and do not return readily. However, when they do return time after time, that can be a sign the fleeting feelings of anxiety have metamorphosed into an anxiety disorder. People who suffer from anxiety disorder also report the following symptoms:

- Muscle tension
- Physical weakness
- Poor memory
- Sweaty hands
- Fear or confusion
- Inability to relax
- Constant worry
- Upset stomach and;
- Poor concentration

Causes & Diagnosis

Anxiety can be caused by several factors that range from external stimuli, shame, emotional abandonment to experiencing an extreme reaction to something that is potentially anxiety-provoking when first exposed to it. Research is yet to explain why some people experience panic attacks or develop phobias, while others who grow up in the same family with shared experiences do not experience the same. The plausible reason for this is that anxiety disorders, like all mental illness, are caused by a set of complex factors that are not yet fully understood. These factors include childhood development, neurobiology, genetics, psychological factors, personality development, including social and environmental cues.

Like most mental disorders, diagnosing anxiety disorders are best performed by a mental health professional — a specialist trained on the nuances of mental disorder diagnoses (such as a psychiatrist or psychologist).

CBT Treatment for Anxiety

Whether you suffer from panic attacks, obsessive thoughts, constant worries, or an incapacitating phobia, it is important to know you do not have to live with anxiety and fear.

Anxiety disorders can be readily treated through a mix of psychotherapy and anti-anxiety medications. Most people taking medications for anxiety disorders do take them on a need-to-use basis, for the specific situation that causes the anxiety reaction.

In some cases, medications play a role in the treatment of **anxiety disorders**. But for most people, therapy alone is the most viable treatment option. The reason for this is that therapy, unlike medication, treats more than just the symptoms of the problem. Therapy can help you to uncover the root cause of your worries and fears, help you learn how to relax, help you look at situations differently in new, less frightening ways, and can help you in developing better coping and problem-solving skills. Therapy provides you with the tools to overcome anxiety and teaches you how to use them **both in the present and in the future.**

Several therapeutic techniques have been designed in treating anxiety, evolving from psychoanalytic approaches to the most widely used and recognized therapy called cognitive behavioral therapy.

Many studies have shown that CBT, as the golden standard, is very effective in the treatment of anxiety ([1](#)).

CBT focuses on:

- Changing unhealthy/ negative thinking that contributes to your anxiety (using cognitive therapy), and;

- Changing your behavior patterns (using behavior therapy) to help you manage the factors that contribute to your anxiety so that you experience less anxiety over time.

Just like depression, several CBT techniques have been developed to address anxiety. However, the leading techniques proven to be very effective against anxiety are:

- Identifying cognitive distortions and cognitive restructuring
- Exposure therapy and;
- Relaxation training such as deep breathing exercises, progressive muscle relaxation, and mindfulness

Although the particular type of anxiety disorder requires the intervention or technique to be individualized or tailored, the anxiety treatments highlighted above, nonetheless, have shown effectiveness for most people with anxiety disorders.

As we deep dive into the aforementioned techniques, kindly refer to Chapter 2 **for an** in-depth **discussion on;** identifying cognitive distortions and cognitive restructuring – this is a **golden standard for all types of** conditions.

Exposure Therapy

It is generally the case that severe anxiety reflects more of worry over the anxiety itself as opposed to the problem underneath.

The Greek philosopher Epictetus said:

"Man is not worried by real problems so much as by his imagined anxieties about real problems." —**Epictetus**

For example, a person with a phobia for public speaking is typically terrified to look like a fool before an audience due to his/her anxiety symptoms (e.g., throwing-up, passing-out, stuttering, sweating, etc.).

Therefore, the real problem is not the fear of public speaking per se, but rather, it is the anticipation of the associated anxiety that causes fear. It is only by confronting such anxiety that people often experience relief. This technique of confronting your anxiety is called **Exposure Therapy** – a behavior-type therapy.

Exposure therapy is a type of CBT technique that is generally considered the best psychological approach in treating anxiety disorders **such as panic disorder, phobia, OCD, PTSD, and SAD**. The primary premise behind exposure therapy is that if you are afraid of something, the best way to conquer it is by going at it head-on (facing your fears). The problem with avoiding your fears is that you will never have the opportunity to overcome them. In fact, avoiding your fears makes them even stronger.

When you are exposed to the source of your anxieties, and nothing terrible happens, the anxiety reduces. This does not mean you should throw yourself (if, for instance, you have a fear of spiders) into a room of tarantulas (a type of spider species) and lock the door, although some have had success with this—it is called "flooding." However, I don't recommend you do this except you really know what you are doing. Instead, you will gradually work your way up to the stimuli you fear.

During exposure therapy, a therapist will slowly introduce you to objects or situations that trigger anxiety or situations you fear. The idea is that when exposed repeatedly, you will feel an increasing sense of control over the situation, thus diminishing your anxiety – this process is called systematic desensitization, and it involves three important parts:

Learning relaxation skills. Your therapist will first teach you a technique for relaxation (this I will show you subsequently), such as deep breathing, progressive muscle relaxation, or mindfulness, which you will have to practice during therapy and at home. Once you start confronting your fears, this relaxation technique will be used to reduce your bodily or physical anxiety response (such as hyperventilating and trembling) and encourage relaxation.

Creating a step-by-step list. Next, you will create a list of about 10 to 20 situations you are scared of, forming a hierarchy that progresses toward your final goal, and ranking them in terms of their intensity, i.e., from the least anxiety-provoking situation to what causes you the most anxiety. For instance, if your final goal is overcoming your fear of flying, you will start the list with "looking at flying airplanes," to "driving with a loved one to the airport," and ending the list with "taking an actual flight with a trusted companion by your side." Each step would be as specific as possible, with a clear and measurable objective.

Exposure (working through the steps). Your therapist will guide you as you work through the list. The goal is to stay put in each scary situation until your fears have subsided. That way, you will learn that you won't be hurt by the feelings of anxiety, thus making them go away. Every time you experience the anxiety becoming too intense, you will turn on the relaxation technique you learned. Once relaxed again, you can then revert your attention to the scary situation. In this way, you will work through each step until you can complete each one without the feeling of being overly distressed.

The exposure to your anxiety-provoking stimuli is usually done in one of three ways in which a therapist can help you in determining the best fit for your situation. The most common are:

- Imaginary exposure: You will be instructed to imagine the feared object or situation vividly. For example, someone who suffers from PTSD might be required to recollect and paint a picture of his/her traumatic experience to help reduce the feelings of fear.

- In-vivo exposure: You will be required to directly face a feared object or situation in real life. For example, someone with a phobia of snakes might be directed to handle a snake, or someone with social anxiety condition might be directed to give a speech before an audience.

- Interoceptive exposure: You might be deliberately exposed to bodily or physical sensations that are harmless, but yet feared. For example, someone with panic attacks might be directed to run to make his/ her heart speed up, and encouraged to maintain contact with the feared sensations – therefore, learning that this sensation is not harmful.

Each of these forms of exposure therapy work for a specific type of anxiety disorder. Thus, in explaining how exposure therapy works using the above, I would streamline the discussion to address specifically how one or more of the above forms can be used to stop panic attacks in its tracks. But before I delve into this, it is important I discuss why success with exposure therapy is not always guaranteed even though it is very effective. Depending on the anxiety disorder being treated, between 10% and 30% of people fail to respond to exposure therapy (Craske, M. G., 1998. *Anxiety disorders: Psychological approaches to theory and treatment*).

While about two-thirds of people follow through with the treatment program to completion, some complete the treatment only to have their fear return afterward. The reason for the failed treatment is often caused by their unwillingness to experience the intense distress associated with an exposure exercise. Also, and perhaps more importantly, many people have not fully grasped the rationale behind exposure-based treatments, thereby making it difficult for them to stick with the treatment when things get tough.

Practicing Exposure Therapy More Effectively

A recent study into the theory of inhibitory learning sheds some light on why some people fail to respond to exposure therapy. As briefly as I can, I will discuss the theory that underpins exposure therapy and review some recent findings from research that can help you practice exposure therapy more effectively to increase its chances of success.

At this point, you have one choice:

- Skip straight to learn and apply the techniques of exposure therapy against panic attacks.
- Read on to learn about the relevant theory first and then learn how these insights can be put into

practice to increase the success rate of exposure therapy and making it more effective.

Habituation: The Backbone of Exposure Therapy

Exposure-based treatments ride on a natural process called habituation. Habituation is when a person, after repeated exposure, stops paying attention or responding to a stimulus, such as an object, thought, person, place, or action.

Examples of habituation can be seen in our everyday life. For instance, when you first moved into a new neighborhood, you may be aggravated by the constant noise of a busy highway running near your house. However, with each day passing by, the noise from the highway fades into the background until you can no longer notice it. In this example, you have become habituated to the sound of the highway.

Another example, but this time, with fear habituation as the goal. In conducting exposure therapy for fear of an object, person, situation, thought, or place, the exposure trial is performed continuously until the person has habituated to a point where he/she reports a significant reduction in fear. For example, if a person with a phobia of spiders reports a fear rating of 8/10 and then afterward, he/ she is presented with a spider, the therapist would wait until the rating of 4/10 or less is reported before terminating the exposure trial. Thus, exposure-based behavior therapies work when habituation to things that are feared is promoted by creating the opportunity to unlearn the associations of dangerous or threatening situations.

Although the above holds as mentioned for habituation, its account, however, of exposure therapy is faulted in some aspects and raises both empirical and pragmatic concerns, the most important of these is that:

- During therapy sessions, habituation does not seem to be necessary for longer-term reduction of fear (Craske, M. G., Kircanski, K., Zelikowsky, M., Mystkowski, J., Chowdhury, N., & Baker, A., 2008. *Optimizing inhibitory learning during exposure therapy. Behaviour Research and Therapy, 46(1), 5-27*). What this means is that even those who do not report reduced fear ratings during an exposure exercise can go on to experience a significant reduction in fear later on. Thus, extinction of fear can happen even if habituation has not happened.

- Stressing the importance of fear reduction during exposure exercise means anxiety is inherently bad and that treatment can only be successful when one is anxiety-free. The implication of this is that people are made to being afraid of fear, causing them to view unexpected but normal surges of fear as signs of failure (Jacoby, R. J., & Abramowitz, J. S., 2016. *Inhibitory learning approaches to exposure therapy: A critical review and translation to obsessive-compulsive disorder. Clinical Psychology Review, 49, 28-40*). A type of CBT, Acceptance, and Commitment Therapy (ACT), has thrown this position into sharp relief.

Are you still surprised about the doubts cast on the overall effectiveness of habituation per exposure exercise? Not to worry because, by the time I am done discussing inhibitory learning theory, which is our next focus, you will better understand why **habituation does not seem to be all too important for exposure therapy to be effective.**

Inhibitory Learning: A Framework for Understanding Exposure

The theory of inhibitory learning was developed to shed light on the process of fear extinction. Fear extinction is the type of learning that happens during exposure therapy when a person confronts his/ her fear-inducing stimulus without experiencing the terrible effects of the fear stimulus. As a result:

- Their expectancies are modified in that they no longer expect the fear-inducing stimulus to result in the terrible consequences of the fear stimulus. For example, a person with a phobia of spiders who handles spiders repeatedly no longer expects spiders to jump at him/ her. Or the person with panic disorder who exposes himself repeatedly to feelings of breathlessness no longer expects to feel that body sensation when he/ she passes out.

- Their behavior is modified in that they approach their fear-inducing stimulus rather than avoid it. For example, a person who completes exposure therapy for social anxiety will no longer dread going for social events and consequently feeling able to be at gatherings with other people in several contexts. And the person with OCD will no longer avoid sharp objects that normally triggered their obsessive thoughts.

Also, the idea behind the inhibitory theory is that the original threat you learned during fear acquisition from an object, person, situation, thought, or place is not replaced or erased by the new learning after you undergo exposure therapy to confront your fears. Instead, the original threat from the object or situation becomes an ambiguous stimulus that lives both in your memory and competes for its retrieval (retrieval competition). This explains why fear can easily return for some people who completed the exposure treatment, while for others, they entirely fail to respond to treatment. Inhibitory learning argues that the reason for this is because the original threat that indicates danger is winning the retrieval competition at that moment and that the new learning that does not indicate danger is not winning, therefore it is not inhibiting the old and original threat.

Figure 12: How fear is learned (fear acquisition)

Inhibitory learning also explains why habituation does not seem all too important for exposure therapy to be effective. This reason for this is not far fetched other than it is the learning that determines the new expectancies and behavior. Inhibitory learning argues that habituation can be good for a person and can be linked with fear extinction, however, what the person learns about the relationship between the fear-inducing stimulus, the terrible effects of the fear stimulus, and about their fear itself, is more important.

What to do to make Exposure Therapy More Effective

In this section, I would discuss some approaches you can take either as a therapist or as an individual to prevent a relapse in treatment and to increase the chances of the new learning winning the retrieval competition, and thus, increasing the chances of success with exposure therapy.

Removal of Safety Signals

It is common to engage in safety behaviors (actions intended to keep us safe or prevent a catastrophe) when we are afraid. However, engaging in safety behaviors, though potentially helpful, can prevent new learning from occurring. For instance, if you have a dog phobia and you employ the safety behavior of being calm when near a dog, you might conclude that: *"It was only OK that time because I remained calm"* instead of a more helpful conclusion: *"Maybe I can be safe around dogs."*

The best advice, in general, is that opportunities for new learning during exposure therapy and the chances of the new learning winning the retrieval competition are more effective when you drop all safety behaviors as fast as possible.

Also, during the exposure trial, double-check that you are not engaging in avoidance by asking *"Is there anything right now I am doing to stop the catastrophe from happening?", "Am I doing anything presently to cope with how I am feeling?"*. Engaging in avoidance prevents the new learning from inhibiting the old and original threat, thus preventing you from achieving success with exposure therapy.

Multiple Contexts

You might have successfully extinguished a fear in a context, such as a therapist's office, just for the fear to reinforce itself in another context when the phobic stimulus is encountered. For example, you suffer from panic attacks but manage to engage in a range of interoceptive exposure exercises with a therapist; however, you find the same exercises challenging while attempting them at home. According to inhibitory learning theory — you might have developed some new learning, but if a fear returns, then the new learning has not won the retrieval competition at that present time.

The solution to this is making more new learning which is more salient, and more easily retrievable, such as:

- Practicing exposure in many contexts.

- Getting out of the therapy room to practice exposure.
- Setting homework (self-practice) tasks and motivating yourself on why you need to complete them.
- Engaging in imaginary, in-vivo, and interoceptive exposures in several places as possible (work, at home, out and about) and at several times of the day / week / year.

Retrieval Cues

The goal of retrieval cues is finding ways to remind you of what you learned during exposure therapy without having to use it as a safety signal. Carrying cues such as a wrist-band to serve as a reminder of prior learning has been demonstrated as helping to convey the beneficial effects of exposure therapy – this helps you to retrieve the new learning when the old and original threat attempts to inhibit the new learning from winning the retrieval competition. Retrieval cues, however, should be used sparingly and as a relapse-prevention skill (keeping alive the hard-won knowledge).

Now that we have discussed and potentially removed any barriers to successfully implementing the exposure therapy, subsequent sections would focus on how to use the exposure therapy technique to stop panic attacks. But before then, let's talk about relaxation training since it is a prerequisite when confronting your fears to help lower your bodily anxiety response (e.g., trembling).

Relaxation Training

Relaxation training is a technique you can use to initiate a calming response within your body. This technique can help people who suffer from a range of mental health conditions, such as anxiety, depression, panic disorder, OCD, and anger, and can it be practised with or without the guidance of a therapist. Although everyone has his/ her own preferences that they find work best for them, however, three of the most commonly used and effective skills for relaxation are deep breathing, progressive muscle relaxation (PMR), and mindfulness. For this section, I would focus on deep breathing and PMR. If you want further guidance on how to practice mindfulness, refer to the mindfulness section of this book.

Deep breathing (diaphragmatic breathing): This technique requires you to take conscious control of your breath. You will learn how to breathe slowly, using your diagram to initiate your body's relaxation response. Although there are many variations to practicing this technique, I will, however, share one easy-to-use method as given below.

Instructions: Deep Breathing

1. Sit comfortably in your chair, and place your hand on your stomach to help you feel the movement of your diaphragm as you breathe.
2. Through your nose, take a deep breath. Breathe in slowly for about 5 seconds.
3. Hold your breath for another 5 seconds. You can do less time if you feel uncomfortable.
4. Slowly release the air for another 5 seconds. You can also do this by puckering your lips while pretending you are blowing through a straw (actually, it can be quite helpful when using a straw for practice).
5. Repeat this process 3 times a day for about 5 minutes, preferably. The more you engage in this practice, the more effective deep breathing will come through for you when you need it.

Deep breathing can be very valuable in the present moment, especially when confronting an anxiety-producing situation or object, or in general, as a way to reduce overall stress. I advise that you practise deep breathing each day even if you are feeling fine—the effects can be long-lasting.

Progressive Muscle Relaxation (PMR): Unlike deep breathing, PMR requires a bit more effort, and it is shown to reduce feelings of stress and anxiety significantly. Although this exercise provides an instant feeling of relaxation, it is, however, best you practice this technique frequently. With experience, you will be able to recognize when you are experiencing tension, and you will possess the skills to help you relax during anxiety or stress-provoking situations. During
PMR exercise, each muscle will be slowly tensed and then relaxed, but not to the point of strain. If you have an injury or pain around your muscles, you can skip the affected area. PMR requires that you pay close attention to the feeling of releasing tension in each of the muscles and the feeling of relaxation that it produces.

Below is the script to get you started in practising PMR:

Lie down or sit back in a comfortable position, and shut your eyes (if you are comfortable with it).

Start by taking a deep breath, notice the feeling of air filling up your lungs, and hold your breath for some seconds.

(brief pause)

Slowly release your breath and allow the tension to leave your body.

Take another deep breath and hold it.

(brief pause)

Again, release the air slowly.

Now even slower, take in another breath, fill up your lungs and hold the air.
(brief pause)

Slowly release your breath and picture the feeling of tension leaving your body.

Now, direct your attention to your feet. Tense your feet by curling your toes, and your foot's arch. Maintain the tension and notice how it feels.

(5 second pause)

Release the tension in your foot, and notice the new feeling of relaxation.

Next, focus on your lower leg, and begin to tense the muscles in your calves. Hold unto them tightly, paying attention to the feeling of tension.

(5 second pause)

Let go of the tension from your lower legs, and again, notice the feeling of relaxation. Continue to take deep breaths.

Next, tense the muscles of your upper leg and pelvis. This can be done by squeezing your thighs tightly together. Ensure sure you feel tenseness without going to the point of strain.

(5 second pause)

Release and feel the tension as it leaves your muscles.

Next, tense your stomach and chest. This can be done by sucking in your stomach. Squeeze harder and hold the tension a little longer.

(5 second pause)

Let go of the tension, and allow your body to go limp. Notice the feeling of relaxation.

Continue to take deep breaths by breathing slowly. Notice the air fill in your lungs, and hold it.

(brief pause)

Slowly release the air, and feel it leaving your lungs.

Next, tense the muscles in your back. This is done by bringing your shoulders together behind you and holding them tightly. Keep holding them as you tense them as hard as possible without straining.

(5 second pause)

Let go of the tension from your back. Feel the tension as it slowly leaves your body and the new feeling of relaxation. Observe as your body feels different when you allow it to relax.

Next, tense your arms all the way up from your hands to your shoulders, make a fist, and squeeze all the way up your arm. Hold it.

(5 second pause)

Let go of the tension from your arms and shoulders, and notice how your fingers, arms, hands, and shoulders feel relaxed. Also, notice the limp feeling and ease in your arms.

Next, go up to your neck and head, and tense your face and neck by distorting the muscles surrounding your eyes and mouth.

(5 second pause)
Let go of the tension, and notice the new feeling of relaxation.

Lastly, tense your entire body – your feet, legs, stomach, chest, arms, neck, and head. Tense a little harder without straining and hold the tension.

(5 second pause)

Let go of the tension, and allow your entire body to go limp. Pay close attention to the feeling of relaxation, and notice the difference from the feeling of tension.

Start waking your body up by moving your muscles slowly. Adjust your arms and legs.

Stretch your muscles, opening your eyes in the process, or when you are ready.

Complementary Therapy for Anxiety

As you begin to explore your anxiety disorder in therapy or through self-administration, you may also feel the need to experiment with complementary therapies that can bring your overall anxiety and stress levels to the barest minimum and help you achieve emotional balance. Just like depression, **Vagus Nerve Stimulation** is one such therapy with increasing popularity that has gained wide acceptance in the treatment of anxiety. Although this approach is typically used in treatment-resistant depression, studies have gone to demonstrate its effectiveness for treatment-resistant anxiety disorders (George, Ward, & Ninan, 2008). Also, studies where the vagus nerve stimulation was used in treating depression, reported significant reductions in anxiety symptoms (Chavel, Westerveld, & Spencer, 2003; Rush, George, & Sackeim et al., 2000).

Dr. Lee Henton, in his book, **_The Secrets of Vagus Nerve Stimulation_**, sheds more light on how the vagus nerve works and its effectiveness as a therapeutic approach in the treatment of anxiety. If you are interested in reading further on the subject of Vagus Nerve Stimulation as an alternative/ complementary therapy for anxiety, then click this [link](https://amzn.to/2Kp4PAK) or use this web address https://amzn.to/2Kp4PAK.

Panic Attacks

A panic attack is a sudden surge of intense fear or discomfort, which feels as though it appeared out of the blue, reaching a peak within minutes (5 to 30 minutes). Panic attacks often involve the feelings of having at least four of the following symptoms:

- Palpitations, accelerated heart rate or pounding heart
- Shaking or trembling
- Sensations of smothering or shortness of breath
- Feeling of choking
- Sweating

- Discomfort or chest pain
- Dizzy feeling, faint or lightheaded
- Heat sensations or chills
- Abdominal distress or nausea
- Tingling or numbness sensations
- Fear of dying
- Feelings of unreality (derealization) or feelings of being detached from oneself (depersonalization) and;
- Fear of going crazy or losing control

Panic attacks are followed by catastrophic thinkings that something bad or terrible is happening or about to happen. Although panic attacks are not dangerous, they, however, do feel terrifying. Some people might experience a one-off panic attack once in a life-time without experiencing another, while some people would go on to experience multiple and constant panic attacks. People who worry about their panic and take steps in preventing the possibility of having another panic attack episode are said to be suffering from panic disorder.

What Causes Panic Attacks?

The cause of panic attacks is not clear, however, no single cause can be attributed to it. Some of the factors that could increase your chances of experiencing panic attacks and panic disorder include:

- **Strong biological reactions to stress:** Some people's bodies respond more to event-producing stress and produce more stress hormones such as cortisol and adrenaline.
- **Anxiety sensitivity:** Some people have high sensitivity compared to others to the feelings in their bodies. More than likely, they tend to notice them and misinterpret them as being dangerous.
- **Other psychological problems:** People that suffer from a wide range of psychological problems mostly experience panic attacks. For example, people with PTSD, OCD, or depression are more likely to experience panic attacks.
- **Genetic factors:** Some people's genetic makeup may be predisposed to developing emotional problems that could result in panic attacks.
- **The use of stimulants:** Some people may develop panic attacks when they abuse the use of stimulants such as amphetamines, caffeine, and cocaine.

What Keeps Panic Attacks Going?

CBT is always very concerned about what keeps a problem going. This is because if you can work out what keeps a problem going, then you can be able to treat it by interrupting the maintenance cycle. David Clark, a psychologist, identified the key maintenance process in panic attacks, and that is: people who experience panic tend to misinterpret the sensations of their body.

How Panic Attacks Develop

To understand how panic attack develops, take a look at the scenario below:

David notices he has a body sensation and says to himself, "my breathing feels cold," then he goes on to have a thought about it "could this be dangerous?" This thought then triggers and apprehensive feeling, which causes him to have anxiety about this feeling, thus strengthening the body sensations, making David to say to himself, "this is really bad." As David pays more attention to his bodily sensations, he becomes even more apprehensive about how he feels, resulting in having even more catastrophic thoughts such as "this is getting even worse," I think I'm going to pass out."

The outcome of this process is that David's misinterpretation of his body sensations would result in feelings of panic reaching its peak.

Other things people who suffer from panic does, which inadvertently prolong their panic disorder are:

- **Looking out for dangerous sensations of the body:** Keeping watch for body sensations is problematic because the more you pay attention to it, the more you are most likely going to experience it.
- **Misinterpreting your body sensations:** Harmless body sensations are most times mistaken to mean an impending catastrophe.
- **Avoiding feared situations or body sensations:** When you avoid situations or things that have to do with panic, it means you will never get to learn how to cope with them or how dangerous they really are. Avoiding situations associated with panic, or using safety behaviors with the intent to prevent a catastrophe are problematic because they not only maintain unhelpful panic related beliefs but also fail to challenge it.
- **Safety-seeking behaviors:** Safety-seeking behaviors are things you do when you try to

prevent a catastrophe from happening. Like avoidance, safety behaviors will prevent you from learning how well you could really cope or how dangerous that situation really is.

Treatment Options for Panic Attacks

One of the core treatment options for panic attacks/panic disorder is CBT, and the technique it uses is exposure therapy. In our previous discussions on how exposure therapy works, we touched on a number of areas to help us better understand how to use this technique in treating anxiety disorders effectively. I also briefly discussed the three major forms of exposure therapy, with each addressing a specific anxiety disorder. These forms are imaginary exposure, in-vivo exposure, and interoceptive exposure (please refer to the section on exposure therapy if you are yet to). Of these forms of therapy, interoceptive exposure is mostly used for panic attacks since it centers on controlling bodily or physical sensations. Hence, our focus would center around how you can use interoceptive exposure to effectively overcome panic attacks. Identifying cognitive distortions and cognitive restructuring are likewise used to treat panic attacks. Please refer to Chapter 2 for an in-depth discussion on this treatment option, which is a **golden standard for all types of conditions.**

Interoceptive Exposure

As early discussed under the **Exposure Therapy** section of this book, interoceptive exposure requires you to be exposed to your feared bodily sensations to elicit the feared reaction, i.e., it will activate any unhelpful beliefs that are associated with the bodily sensations, maintains the sensations with no distraction or avoidance, and then allows new learning about the sensations to occur. Because the trigger for panic attacks in the context of panic disorder is the body, the focus of the exposure exercises is on the anxiety symptoms themselves. Thus, the goal of this technique is to help you not only see that the symptoms of panic are unharmful, though uncomfortable, but also to help you cope with your panic attacks and effectively put a stop to it.

Without further ado, let's take a look at how to put the exposure exercise into practice. But first, below are a number of interoceptive exposure exercises that you can use to toughen up against the probability of experiencing a panic attack. It is important that you practice one exercise daily after attempting a number of them to find the one that will trigger some anxiety. This is because each person may not respond the same way to the same exercise.

Symptom - Dizziness or lightheadedness

- Spin for 1 minute in a swivel chair, then take a 1 minute break. Repeat this 8 times.

- For 30 seconds, shake head from side to side, then take a 30 second break. Repeat this 15 times.

- Bend over and place head in-between the legs for 30 seconds while sitting, then quickly sit up. Repeat this 15 times.

- Hyperventilate (shallow breathing at a rate of 100-120 breaths per minute) for 1 minute, then breathe normally for another 1 minute. Repeat this 8 times.

Symptom - Derealization

- For 1 minute, stare at a light on the ceiling, then try reading for 1 minute. Repeat this 8 times.

- Stare at yourself in a mirror for 3 minutes, then one minute break. Repeat this 3 times.

- For 3 minutes, stare at a small dot (like the size of a dime) posted on the wall.

- For 2 minutes, stare at an optical illusion (such as a "psychedelic" rotating screen saver, rotating spiral, etc.), then break for one minute. Repeat this 5 times.

Symptom - Tightness in throat

Wear a scarf, tie, or turtleneck shirt tightly around your neck for 5 minutes, take 1 minute break. Repeat this 3 times.

Symptm - Rapid heartbeat

Run up and downstairs, or on the spot for 1 minute, then take a 1 minute break. Repeat this 8 times.

Symptom - Breathlessness or smothering feelings

- For 30 seconds, hold your breath, then breathe normally for another 30 seconds. Repeat this 15 times.

- For 2 minutes, breathe through a small narrow straw (plug your nose if necessary), then breathe normally for 1 minute. Repeat this 5 times.

- Sit with your head covered by a heavy blanket or coat.

Symptom - Choking feelings, gag reflex

For a few seconds or until a gag reflex is induced, place a tongue depressor or a smooth unharmful object such as a brush on the back of your tongue. Repeat this for 15 minutes.

Symptom - Trembling or shaking

For 60 seconds, tense all the muscles in your body or hold a push-up position for as long as you can, then break for another 60 seconds. Repeat this 8 times.

Symptom - Sweating

- Sit in a hot car, a hot, stuffy room, or a small room with a space heater)

- Take a hot drink

Using the interoceptive exercises above as well as the steps of systemic desensitization as discussed under the exposure therapy section, let's see what an interoceptive exposure for panic attacks would look like using the experience of Jane, who suffers from panic attacks.

Jane is a 30-year-old woman with a panic disorder. She experiences panic attacks that appear out of the blues, often worrying about having another panic attack episode. In some cases, she feels a little anxious, and starts to feel dizzy, thus making her worry the panic attack might get worse; and yes, it usually does. Jane decides to visit a therapist who immediately identified the interoceptive exposure exercise as one of the suitable treatment options to address the bodily sensations that cause her to panic. Below is a step by step process Jane underwent with the help of her therapist.

Step One: Pick a Trigger

To begin the exercise, Jane chooses to start with the "dizziness" trigger, because it is most often the body sensation that triggers the panicky thoughts fueling the anxiety and making it worse.

Step Two: Create a Fear Hierarchy

Using the list her therapist gave her, Jane went on to list the different interoceptive exercises that she can use to trigger some anxiety.

Exposure exercise (ways to trigger the anxiety)

- Spin for 1 minute in a swivel chair, then 1 minute break. Repeat this 8 times.

- For 30 seconds, shake head from side to side, then 30 second break. Repeat this 15 times.

- Bend over and place head in-between the legs for 30 seconds while sitting, then quickly sit up. Repeat this 15 times.

- Hyperventilate (shallow breathing at a rate of 100-120 breaths per minute) for 1 minute, then breathe normally for another 1 minute. Repeat this 8 times.

Step Three: Rate the Hierarchy

Using a scale of 0-10 (a Subjective Units of Distress Scale: SUDS), Jane rates the level of anxiety/distress about the sensations for each exercise, where 0 is the lowest, and 10 the highest.

Exposure Exercise	*Anxiety Rating*
- Spin for 1 minute in a swivel chair, Then take a 1 minute break. Repeat this 8 times.	7
- For 30 seconds, shake your head from side to side, then 30 second break. Repeat this 15 times.	9
- Bend over and place head in-between the legs for 30 seconds while sitting, then quickly sit up. Repeat this 15 times.	7
- Hyperventilate (shallow breathing at a rate of 100-120 breaths per minute) for 1 minute, then breathe normally for another 1 minute. Repeat this 8 times	5

SUDS		
Rating	Meaning	Comment
0	Relaxed	You feel no distress. You feel calm.
1-4	Mild	You feel like you are more nervous or alert, but you can still cope.
5-6	Moderate	It is becoming difficult for you to cope with. You are distracted by anxiety and might use safety behaviors or avoidance.
7-8	High	It is difficult to cope with. You are having difficulties concentrating, and you are looking to escape.
9-10	Severe to extreme	You can't cope. The response of your body is extremely overwhelming that you think you cannot stay in the situation any longer.

Step Four: Starting Exposure

In the 5-6 range on the SUDS, Jane picks an exposure exercise item from the list. She begins her practice of hyperventilating for 1 minute, then takes a 1 minute break, repeating it 8 times – which takes her about 16 minutes to complete. Whenever she experiences severe fear of her panic attacks in the process of undertaking this exercise, she quickly practised the relaxation training skills she learned on deep breathing, which helped to lower her bodily anxiety response. She uses the SUDS to track her progress by rating her anxiety level before and after the exposure.

Step Five: Middle Sessions of Exposure

Once Jane feels like her anxiety level for the hyperventilation exercise has reduced to around a "3", she then moves to the next harder exercise on the hierarchy. She continues practising these exercises daily and keeps moving up the hierarchy until she gets accustomed to the feeling of lightheadedness or dizziness, as well as being more at peace with the probability that she might have a panic attack when she feels lightheaded or dizzy.

Since she is also worried when the feeling of tightness is experienced in her throat, Jane decided to go through some of the interoceptive exercises for this sensation as well. Jane and her therapist, along with her exposure practice, worked on some of the thoughts that tend to fuel the anxiety once it is triggered. Please refer to Chapter 2 on the section of identifying cognitive distortions and cognitive restructuring to learn more about how negative thoughts can be identified and reframed.

Step Six: Ending Exposure

Jane continues practising the exposure exercises for about 10 weeks, changing the exercise for about each week as she moved up the hierarchy. This, with a combination of cognitive skills, improved her panic symptoms and made her feel confident enough to manage a panic attack that might occur in the future.

Exercise

Following the steps Jane went through in confronting the body sensations that caused her to experience panic attacks, use the table below to document your journey. But before you begin, kindly pay attention to the following.

Precautions

It is essential that you take note of the following before attempting any of the exposure exercises.

1. You must be physically healthy before starting or completing the exercises. If you have any health challenges that might be complicated by the physical strain from the exercises, then you should either not take the exercise, or discontinue

the exercise, whichever comes first. Some of the health challenges include:

- Epilepsy or seizures
- A heart condition
- Pregnancy
- Physical injuries, e.g., neck problem
- History of fainting/ low blood pressure

Check with your therapist/ doctor to determine if you can proceed with the exposure exercises given your condition.

2. Although exposure exercises are typically performed with the guidance of a therapist or a mental health professional, conducting these exposure exercises on your own is most times the best way to challenge or confront your beliefs about body sensations. However, if you find any exercises particularly difficult, or you are concerned about your progress, please get in touch with a therapist or a licensed mental health practitioner to guide you through the process.

Preparation for the tasks

Ensure you try to trigger all the body sensations or symptoms using the interoceptive exercises highlighted underneath each sensation. This will help you determine which body sensations and exercises are relevant to you or that causes you to panic so that you know which of them to focus on.

Below are a few hints to help you as you prepare for the exercises.

1. Talking to a trusted or supportive friend or relative about the tasks you are doing can be helpful. Perhaps you can regularly talk with them to discuss your progress and if you are having any challenges. This can help you in acknowledging the positive steps being taken and can serve as a motivation for you to continue.

2. The exercises are not in any particular order. However, it is best you start with the exercises that have the lowest anxiety rating and gradually move up the hierarchy. This way, you won't be so overwhelmed and decide to use safety behaviors or avoidance to discontinue the exercise.

3. Write down which exercise(s) you will complete each day, and create an appointment to perform

the exercises by blocking out a time that is convenient for you on your calendar. This will help you in formalizing your commitment to doing it. Ensure that you set aside enough time to complete at least 1 exercise every day.

Performing the tasks

1. Experience the sensations as much as you can and avoid using safety behaviors or avoidance to distract yourself from the sensations. Take note of the ways you can subtly avoid these sensations. Common methods of avoidance include:

    - Stopping the task early. For instance, when you are thinking, "That's enough, my heart is beating faster."

    - Not properly completing the tasks. For instance, when you are attempting to trigger the sensation of sweating through heat, you partly open the window, which is a subtle form of avoidance.

    - Distracting yourself from paying attention to the sensations instead of paying full attention to them.

2. During the exercises, use disputation (refer to Chapter 2 on cognitive restructuring) to confront or challenge any catastrophic/ negative thoughts about the sensations you experience. Perhaps you can make a flashcard and have it close by.

3. Whenever you experience fear of panic attacks in the process of undergoing an exercise, quickly apply the relaxation training skills you learned to help you confront your fears and lower your bodily anxiety response.

4. Although experiencing some sensation is better than nothing, ensure you complete the full exercise – this will provide you with a more accurate assessment of the fear of your sensation.

5. In some exercises, the sensations can develop during the exercise, while in others, they develop shortly after the exercise. So, ensure you pay full attention to the sensations that take place during and after the exercise.

6. After each exercise, make some notes about your experience using SUDS.

Ongoing exposure

Working through an exposure session is very critical if you want to get used to the feared sensations. To keep moving onwards and upwards, below are a few hints to help you with the process of moving through all of your feared sensations.

- **Repetition:** It is important that you repeat each exercise until your SUDS rating decreases to less than 5. This can be done later on the same day, or you can have it scheduled for the next day or so.

- **Acknowledge your achievements:** After completing an exposure session, ensure that you reward yourself for your efforts. The reward should be something you find positive and encouraging in recognition of your achievements.

- **Use your resources:** Talk to a trusted relative or friend or even your therapist about your progress, and work through any unhelpful thoughts you might have concerning the completion of the exercises.

Exercise	Before Exercise SUDS (0-10)	After Exercise SUDS (0-10)	Symptoms & Thoughts What did you notice in your body? What went through your mind?
Dizziness or lightheadedness - Spin for 1 minute in a swivel chair, then take a 1 minute break. Repeat this 8 times. - For 30 seconds, shake your head from side to side, then 30 second break. Repeat this 15 times.			

- Bend over and place head in-between the legs for 30 seconds while sitting, then quickly sit up. Repeat this 15 times. - Hyperventilate (shallow breathing at a rate of 100-120 breaths per minute) for 1 minute, then breathe normally for another 1 minute. Repeat this 8 times.			
Derealization - For 1 minute, stare at a light on the ceiling, then try reading for 1 minute. Repeat this 8 times. - Stare at yourself in a mirror for 3 minutes, then one minute break.			

Repeat this 3 times. - For 3 minutes, stare at a small dot (like the size of a dime) posted on the wall. - For 2 minutes, stare at an optical illusion (such as a "psychedelic" rotating screen saver, rotating spiral, etc.), then break for one minute. Repeat this 5 times.			
Tightness in throat Wear a scarf, tie, or turtleneck shirt tightly around your neck for 5 minutes, take one minute break. Repeat this 3 times.			
Rapid heartbeat Run up and downstairs, or on the spot for 1 minute, then take a 1 minute break. Repeat this 8 times.			

Choking feelings, gag reflex For a few seconds or until a gag reflex is induced, place a tongue depressor or a smooth unharmful object such as a brush on the back of your tongue. Repeat this for 15 minutes.			
Trembling or shaking For 60 seconds, tense all the muscles in your body or hold a push-up position for as long as you can, then break for another 60 seconds. Repeat this 8 times.			
Sweating - Sit in a hot car, a hot, stuffy room, or a small room with a space heater) - Take a hot drink			

Breathlessness or smothering feelings - For 30 seconds, hold your breath, then breathe normally for another 30 seconds. Repeat this 15 times. - For 2 minutes, breathe through a small narrow straw (plug your nose if necessary), then breathe normally for 1 minute. Repeat this 5 times. - Sit with your head covered by a heavy blanket or coat.			

The end… almost!

Hey! We've made it to the final chapter of this book, and I hope you've enjoyed it so far.

If you have not done so yet, I would be incredibly thankful if you could take just a minute to leave a quick review on the product page of this book.

Reviews are not easy to come by, and as an independent author with a little marketing budget, I rely on you, my readers, to leave a short review on the product page of this book

Even if it is just a sentence or two!

So if you really enjoyed this book, please… leave a brief review on the product page of this book.

I truly appreciate your effort to leave your review, as it truly makes a huge difference.

Thanks once again from the depth of my heart for purchasing this book and reading it to the end.

Chapter 5

CBT for Anger Management

What is Anger?

Anger is a natural response to threats that can either inspire us to confront injustice or problematic situations or can motivate us to protect ourselves when attacked. The fact is, everyone gets angry, and this is normal. However, there is a need for us to manage our anger. Common sense and social norms tell us that we cannot lash out each time we get irritated or upset.

Anger varies in intensity, i.e., what causes one person to be mildly irritated might trigger an intense rage in someone else. Similarly, people express anger differently. While some verbally express their anger by shouting, swearing, name-calling, or making threats, others become violent by hitting or pushing others or even by breaking things they lay their hands on. Also, some people express their anger in passive ways, for instance, by sulking or ignoring others. Other people may bottle up when they feel very angry or even turn it against themselves by self-harming.

At this point, I need to mention that anger and aggression are not one and the same. While anger is an emotion that we feel, aggression, on the other hand, is the behavior that, in some cases, stems from the thoughts and feelings of anger. In other words, you can be angry but choose not to be aggressive.

Angry Thoughts, Behaviors, and Physical Symptoms

Anger tends to be associated with the thoughts of hostility, maladaptive behaviors, and physiological arousal. Thoughts most times, focuses on the perceived rights and wrongs and a feeling or sense of injustice (such as 'I'm being disrespected'; 'I'm badly/unfairly treated,' 'I'm being disappointed again,' 'They're making a mockery of me' etc.). In other cases, it is often a sense that others have fallen short of your expectations, or standards (such as 'This isn't good enough'; 'I won't accept this,' 'I can't trust anyone' etc.).

The physical consequence of anger is that it results in physiological changes. Your blood pressure and heart rate go up, and your adrenaline level rises. Anger can also impair your concentration and memory capability. Other physical symptoms that are noticeable from an angry person include teeth or fist clenching, stomach-churning/butterflies, tense muscles, and shaking, amongst others.

When angry, you might feel restless, on edge, tense, or uptight. You might also feel the urge to hit out, ignore or not talk to a person, shout or argue, make sarcastic comments, or even storm away from a situation.

The Cycle of Anger – How Anger Develops

An episode of anger display begins from ground zero and gradually builds up, or rapidly via three stages. Here we will discuss these stages alongside the actions associated with them.

- **Escalation** – At this stage, you begin to receive several cues our mind and body alert us to about the build-up of anger from the inside. These cues include physical (heavy breathing), cognitive (thoughts of revenge), emotional (guilt), or behavioral (teeth-clenching).

- **Expression** – Should the phase of escalation go unattended, the expression phase will follow suit shortly. A violent display of anger is characterized by this, which may include physical or verbal aggression.

- **Post-expression** – At this stage, you begin to realize the negative consequences of your physical or verbal aggressiveness. This could be inner feelings of guilt, regret, shame to external consequences such as retribution, or arrest from others.

Everyone has his/ her personal intensity, duration, and frequency of anger in the anger cycle. For instance, someone may get angry in just a few minutes, while another may escalate gradually with time before hitting the expression stage. The goal of CBT is to prevent anyone from reaching the expression stage. With the use of CBT techniques and practices, anger can be identified and managed before it reaches the escalation stage.

Causes of Anger

- **Family background**: People who easily get angry may come from a chaotic or difficult family background. They may have never been encouraged nor learned to express how they feel healthily. A person who is/ was emotionally deprived (for example, not being nurtured when young, or not receiving empathy) and punitive parenting (being frequently shamed, invalidated, or criticized) can lead to low self-esteem, mistrust, and anger.

- **Negative thinking style**: Difficult situations or events can lead to a negative thinking style, which then becomes ingrained with time and becomes a part of one's outlook on life. Negative thinking can turn into a bad habit, so much that you are not aware your thinking style is becoming excessively negative and how it is affecting your day-day life. Unsurprisingly, a continuous negative outlook can result in anger problems.

- **Low tolerance for frustration:** Some people laugh off or forget about minor frustrations from everyday life (such as traffic jams, a poor internet, or phone connection, unfriendly shopkeepers, etc.), and others find it difficult letting go and may even end up fuming hours later. People who get angry easily tend to have what is called a low tolerance for frustration. One's genes and environment/ upbringing are factors that can influence if you have a low tolerance for frustration. Frustrations are part and parcel of life, so toughening up your tolerance level is an essential part of anger management.

- **Stress:** Stressful life events such as abuse or being bullied, divorce, or separated, financial problems, work pressures, and job loss can drive one to anger.

Cost of Anger

- Some people think 'letting it all out' is a good way of getting the anger out of their system. Studies show that doing so, in fact, does escalate the anger and aggression levels.

- Anger hurts relationships, whether it is family, romantic, friendship, or professional. 'You are always messing things up!' 'This damn machine does not work,' – these types of black-and-white statements can upset and alienate the person who hears them, thereby making them less inclined to help you.

- Anger disrupts your thinking patterns. Instead of trying to resolve problems calmly, anger exaggerates them. This can briefly fortify your self-esteem and make you feel your anger is justified, but ultimately, it fosters feelings of hopelessness, making resolvable problems seem unresolvable.

- People most times feel very badly about themselves after having an angry outburst, resulting in feelings of guilt and shame.

Myths & Facts About Anger

Several widespread beliefs and myths exist concerning anger. Let's deconstruct these myths to see what the facts are.

Myth 1 – Venting out my anger relaxes me. It isn't healthy holding it in.

Fact – Holding on to anger is like you holding in your palms red-hot coals. Anger should be expressed, but not by being aggressive because aggressiveness will only result in further confrontations.

Myth 2 – My aggressive behavior gives me the attention, obedience, and respect I deserve

Fact – Understanding someone and not by intimidation lies the power to influence. People may submit to you out of being bullied, but they won't give you the respect you seek, and eventually, you will be deserted if you are unable to accept opposing viewpoints.

Myth 3 – I cannot control my anger.

Fact – Anger, like any other emotion, is also a result of the situation you are in. Assessing the situation from multiple perspectives prevents misjudgment and anger.

Myth 4 – Suppressing your anger is all about anger management.

Fact – Anger is neither to be suppressed nor vented out, instead, it should be expressed in a manner that is non-violent and constructive. This is what Anger Management is all about.

CBT Treatment for Anger

CBT teaches us that how we behave when we are angry depends on our ability to manage our feelings and express our emotions.

In cognitive behavioral therapy, your therapist will:

- Help you understand the events/ situations and your interpretations of those situations that led to your feelings of anger.

- Help you in identifying possible distortions in how you think about a situation, and challenge you to uncover the validity of these distortions.

- Help you to reframe the thoughts into more balanced and adaptive ("cool") thoughts.

To achieve the above, I would use the Albert Ellis A-B-C-D technique, who is credited as one of the pioneers of CBT. This technique employs the use of thought records in challenging distorted or irrational thinkings about a situation and reconstructing them into more realistic and rational ones.

Another well-known technique is relaxation training, which includes deep breathing, progressive muscle relaxation, and mindfulness, all of which are proven methods in managing anger. In chapter 4 of this book, I discussed the relaxation training technique. Kindly refer to this section if you haven't yet done so.

Ellis's A-B-C-D Technique

The A-B-C-D model is a classic **CBT** technique which, when applied effectively, can help in addressing several emotional difficulties, including anger management problems. In chapter 1 of this book, I briefly touched on this model as a type of CBT. However, I would go deeper into explaining how this model can be applied to anger management.

Below is an overview of what the A-B-C-D model looks like, using anger as the problem focus:

A = Activating Event

This is the situation or trigger that stirs up your anger.

B = Belief System

This refers to your interpretation of the activating event (A) such as *"What are your beliefs and expectations of other people's behavior?" "What is it you tell yourself about what occurred?"* In chapter 2 of this book, I discussed the belief system extensively and how to identify your core beliefs about a situation/ problem. Please refer to this chapter if you are yet to do so.

C = Consequences

This refers to how you feel and what you do per your belief system, i.e., the emotional and behavioral consequences resulting from A + B. When angry, it is also typical to feel other emotions such as fear. Other consequences that may arise include clenching your fists, feeling warm, and taking more shallow breaths. More dramatic behavioral consequences include name-calling, yelling, and physical violence.

D = Dispute

This is a critical step in the anger management process. This requires that you examine your belief system and expectations. This step helps you question if your beliefs and expectations are unrealistic or irrational? And if so, what would a calmer and alternative way to relate to the situation be? By disputing those knee-jerk beliefs, you can then begin to take a more rational and balanced approach toward the situation, which can help you control your anger.

In summary, this step aims to identify cognitive distortions in your thinking and how it can be restructured into more balanced thoughts. I discussed extensively on this in [Chapter 2](). You can refer to this chapter for more in-depth details. However, in this section, using an example, I would discuss as clearly as possible how to identify distorted or unrealistic thinking and how to dispute your distorted thoughts or expectations and reframe them into more realistic ones.

Example of the A-B-C-D Model

Let's take a look at an example as I describe how this model can be applied to anger management.

A = Activating Event

You are driving to work, and you get cut off by somebody, almost resulting in a collision. To begin with, you were already feeling worn out because you were running late to work and had a big day ahead of you.

B = Belief System

You think to yourself, "people should not drive in such a way like that," "I'm a very courteous driver, and I don't drive like that," "every driver on the road these days are reckless," "if I had been hit by that car, I would have been so late to work, or it could have been even worse, I could have gotten injured."

C = Consequences

After the event that triggered your beliefs (i.e., being cut-off in traffic), you then rolled down your window and exploded in anger at the other driver. You observe your muscles becoming tensed, your heart beats rapidly, and you feel like hitting the steering wheel. You also notice you feel some elements of fear.

D = Dispute

In responding to the situation that triggered your anger, instead of reinforcing the thoughts that fuel your anger, you could instead, reconstruct your thinking (this is the dispute part of the model). For instance, you could say to yourself:

"It is disappointing that some people drive so recklessly, but that is just how life is. Most people actually do adhere to road safety rules, and I'm glad I do as well. Probably that driver had an emergency he was responding to, or probably not, but you'll never know. It was scary to have almost gotten hit. Still, even if we got into a fender bender, I would have, nonetheless, gotten to work, and probably nothing serious would have occurred because of it."

As you can see, applying this type of rational thinking and self-talk is most likely going to diffuse some of the anger and help you relax and remain calm.

Although using the A-B-C-D model is a good practice even though it is after the fact, it is, however, reflective of the process that helps to rewire your brain and retrain your mind by increasing your awareness of patterns in your thoughts and the situations, and ways you can respond to them more effectively. For example, you may begin noticing that there are similar situations that constantly bring up anger for you. Essentially, these are areas of vulnerability you need to be aware of and work hard on.

Most times, after an angry incident, people get insight into what just happened and regretting what they said or did. But, at the time, things just happen to escalate so quickly. This added level of awareness can really help you slow down a bit – a key factor in anger management. Being able to take a pause, breathe deeply, and then deciding how to respond instead of reacting to the situation can help prevent the negative consequences of your anger.

P.S: The ABCD model in the context described above can likewise be applied to depression and anxiety disorders.

Exercise

Using the ABCD Model to Manage Your Anger

The first step toward using this anger management tool is by increasing your awareness of what is going on in each step. To begin this exercise, review each of the following:

- Identify what situation or event that triggered your anger.

- Reflect on your beliefs/ response to the triggering situation (e.g., what did you say about it to yourself).

- Identify all the emotional and behavioral responses that ensued.

Because our minds are fast-paced, we can get to the consequence C very quickly. So, to begin applying this model, it would also be helpful that you do some analyses of previous situations that have triggered your anger by noting them down in each category. To help you with this task, use the thought record below:

A = Activating Agent	B = Beliefs	C = Consequence	D = Dispute
The situation or trigger that made you angry	Your interpretation of the trigger; what you say about it to yourself	How you felt and what you did about your response to your beliefs; the emotional and behavioral consequences from A + B	Examine your beliefs and expectations. Are they irrational or unrealistic? If so, what other ways can you relate to the situation

Taking your time to write out these steps can really help you in getting this learning into your subconscious mind so that you can draw upon it later on in the heat of the moment. In other words, doing this can help with your practice of anger management, especially when reviewing previous incidents and coming up with more balanced and positive solutions that can help in calming you down, instead of fueling the anger.

After writing down the A-B-Cs, complete the D-dispute section by identifying more rational, realistic, and balanced things you can rather say to yourself about the situation. Likewise, you can include specific behaviors in this section. For instance, you might want to write down reminders as a note to yourself, such as "count to 10 before making any utterances" or "take some deep breaths."

Conclusion

I'd like to thank and congratulate you for transiting the lines of this book from start to finish.

I hope this book helped in providing you with a clearer understanding of what cognitive behavioral therapy (CBT) is all about and how important this therapeutic approach can be to your mental health and emotional wellbeing. In this book, I showed factual evidence to support the effectiveness of CBT in treating several health conditions that include depression, anxiety, anger, and panic attacks and likewise, I discussed to a great extent the proven CBT techniques you can apply right away to get your mental health and overall wellbeing in the right state and shape. These techniques in no particular order include how to identify distortions in your thinking and how to challenge and replace them with more rational thoughts, how to use behavioral activation to overcome depression, how to use exposure therapy to end anxiety, how to use relaxation training skills such as deep breathing and mindfulness, and specifically, how to use interoceptive exposure therapy to stop panic attacks in its tracks. I also showed you how to use the A-B-C-D technique to manage your anger and get your emotions under control. Above all else and most importantly, I hope that you found these techniques to be quite insightful and useful either as a therapist seeking additional knowledge in your profession or as someone looking for ways to exercise control over his/her mental health.

At this point onward, you are now equipped to lend better therapeutic advice to your patient or able to take better control of your health. The next step is to apply the techniques discussed, which this book has demonstrated as invaluable. So, I urge you to feel free to experiment with these techniques right away without hesitation. Personally, most of what I have shared and discussed were the steps I took toward reclaiming my health from when I was once depressed, anxious, and angry about everything, and because I know how powerful these techniques were in helping me break the hold these vicious emotions had on me, I too want you to break the hold they have on you or your patient.

Finally, I want you to take personal responsibility for your health and wellbeing by incorporating the tips I have shared in this book into your daily life routine. No one can do this for you, except you.

Remember…

"Knowing is not enough; we must apply. Willing is not enough; we must do" – Goethe.

I wish you the very best on your journey toward health and wellness!

References

Whalley, M. H. K. (2020, July 5). What is Cognitive Behavioral Therapy (CBT)? Retrieved from https://www.psychologytools.com/self-help/what-is-cbt/

Ben Martin, P., 2020. In-Depth: Cognitive Behavioral Therapy. Psych Central. Available at: <https://psychcentral.com/lib/in-depth-cognitive-behavioral-therapy/>

Suffolkcognitivetherapy.com. 2020. Types Of CBT | Suffolk Cognitive-Behavioral, PLLC. Available at: <http://suffolkcognitivetherapy.com/web/specialties/types-of-cbt/>

Whalley, M. H. K. (2020b, July 5). What is Cognitive Behavioral Therapy (CBT)? Retrieved from https://www.psychologytools.com/self-help/what-is-cbt/

Eddins, R. M. (2020, June 19). Feeling Anxious or Depressed? Watch Out for Cognitive Distortions.

Retrieved from https://eddinscounseling.com/types-of-cognitive-distortions/

Grohol, J. P. M. (2020, July 6). Depression. Retrieved from https://psychcentral.com/depression/

Williams, A. (2015, July 9). Core Beliefs Part 1: Identifying and Understanding Core Beliefs. Retrieved from https://www.rowancenterla.com/new-blog/2015/7/9/core-beliefs-part-1-identifying-and-understanding-core-beliefs

Psychology Tools. 2020. Delivering More Effective Exposure Therapy In CBT - Psychology Tools. Available at:<https://www.psychologytools.com/articles/delivering-more-effective-exposure-therapy-in-cbt/>

Eddins, R. M. (2020b, June 19). Identifying and Changing Your Core Beliefs | Learn How CBT Can Help. Retrieved from https://eddinscounseling.com/uncover-core-beliefs-can-change/

Therapy, H. (2019, October 19). Core Beliefs in CBT - Identifying And Analysing Personal Beliefs. Retrieved from https://www.harleytherapy.co.uk/counselling/core-beliefs-cbt.htm

Cognitive behavioral therapy in anxiety disorders: current state of the evidence. (2011, December 1). Retrieved from https://www.ncbi.nlm.nih.gov/pmc/articles/PMC3263389/

Grohol, J. P. M. (2020a, July 6). Anxiety Disorders. Retrieved from https://psychcentral.com/anxiety/

Treated, P. and management, A., 2020. CBT Cork | Anger Management.| Kinsale CBT. Available at: <https://www.kinsalecbt.com/anger-management/>

Pratt, K. L. (2017, May 12). Psychology Tools: A-B-C-D Model for Anger Management. Retrieved from https://healthypsych.com/psychology-tools-a-b-c-d-model-for-anger-management/

www.ingramcontent.com/pod-product-compliance
Lightning Source LLC
Chambersburg PA
CBHW050317120526
44592CB00014B/1941